BUTTERFLY GARDENS

LURING NATURE'S

LOVELIEST

POLLINATORS

TO YOUR YARD

Alcinda Lewis, Guest Editor

D1166291

FOR THE ADVANCE-MENT OF BOTANY AND THE SERVICE OF THE CITY

BROOKLYN BOTANIC GARDEN PUBLICATIONS · MCMXCV ·

Janet Marinelli
SERIES EDITOR

Anne Witte Garland
ASSOCIATE EDITOR

Bekka Lindstrom
ART DIRECTOR

Stephen K·M. Tim
VICE PRESIDENT, SCIENCE, LIBRARY & PUBLICATIONS

Judith D. Zuk
PRESIDENT

Elizabeth Scholtz
DIRECTOR EMERITUS

Handbook #143

Copyright © Summer 1995, 1996, 1997 by the Brooklyn Botanic Garden, Inc.

BBG gardening books are published quarterly at 1000 Washington Ave., Brooklyn, NY 11225

Subscription included in Brooklyn Botanic Garden membership dues ($35.00 per year)

ISSN 0362-5850 ISBN # 0-945352-88-3

PRINTED IN KOREA

Cover photograph: Coral Hairstreak on butterfly weed

Table of Contents

GARDEN "PUBS" FOR BUTTERFLIES

BY ALCINDA LEWIS

LIKE MOST GARDENERS, I take such pleasure in flowers that I lose sight of the fact that they did not evolve solely to bring me happiness. As we all know but usually forget, flowers exist first and foremost to attract pollinating insects. Some of the most intriguing pollinators are the butterflies, which grace our gardens with their unique beauty and magic. As you'll see in this book, to attract butterflies we need to make only relatively small changes in our current practices and styles. The result can be gardens that require less labor but provide more enjoyment.

Several years ago, I lived and worked for a few months on the estate of British biologist Miriam Rothschild, an early promoter of butterfly gardening. I arrived in late winter to an unkempt, seemingly chaotic assortment of gardens, fields and medieval woods. But as spring unfolded and flowers appeared everywhere, I saw the method in this apparent madness. Wildflowers were combined in lovely tapestries with prized horticultural varieties, and plants that butterflies love were intermingled with the roses they ignore.

As Rothschild demonstrated in her book *The Butterfly Gardener* (Michael Joseph, London, 1983), we can attract butterflies by providing a garden "pub"— by growing the nectar-producing flowers they prefer. Creating such a butterfly pub is the subject of this book, from an introduction to butterfly biology and the principles of butterfly gardens, to detailed encyclopedias of common butterflies and their nectar plants.

As you succeed in attracting butterflies to your garden, you will also want to give them incentives to linger. For this, you'll need to provide food for their young. Food plants for butterfly larvae are not necessarily the same as nectar plants for adults, and they are not covered extensively in this book. We do list larval plants in the butterfly encyclopedia and provide leads to further information on this second stage of butterfly gardening in the bibliography.

One not-so-hidden agenda of many advocates of butterfly gardening is conservation. Jennifer Owen, in her book *The Ecology of a Garden* (University Press, Cambridge, 1991), argues that even small, conventional gardens can be a significant collective nature reserve, particularly in urban areas. Even if conservation isn't your primary goal, you can take some satisfaction in knowing that your efforts may be contributing to the preservation of some of the world's most beautiful creatures.

As with so many endeavors, these worthy reasons for butterfly gardening coexist with ones grounded in human pleasure and excitement. Jo Brewer, one of the first proponents of butterfly gardening in this country, recognized this when she wrote, "A garden is as static as a painting until butterflies bring it to life."

BUTTERFLY BIOLOGY FOR GARDENERS

BY ALCINDA LEWIS

WATCHING BUTTERFLIES in an English meadow, the 19th century biologist R. M. Christy concluded, "I have seldom seen one whose flight gave me the idea that the insect had the least notion as to where it was going." This is part of the appeal of butterflies: They symbolize lazy summer days, largely because of their seemingly aimless flight. But nothing could be further from the truth. Butterflies are not only purposeful but also frenetically busy, focused on concrete objectives and beset by countless obstacles.

From almost the minute their wings harden, newly emerged males begin searching for mates. Females must search for specific food plants for their progeny (see "The Life Cycle of a Butterfly," page 8). These activities are fueled by nectar, requiring a time-consuming search for suitable plants. Males of many species must also find mud puddles or dung—sources of additional nutrients, the salts that plants lack. And because butterflies are cold-blooded, all of this activity is limited to times of warm sunshine.

Butterflies' quests can be difficult for many reasons. Males must find females of the same species among all the butterflies flying at the time. As the females search for the particular plants on which to lay their eggs, they are constantly interrupted by courting males. And the right plant needs to be in a sunny spot and of acceptable quality or quantity.

Eastern Tailed Blues mating. From almost the minute their wings harden, male butterflies begin searching for a mate.

6

Like many butterfly species, the Two-tailed Swallowtail seeks out necessary nutrients in puddles and dung.

The Monarch, for example, uses primarily members of the milkweed family as a larval food. Once the female lays an egg, the larva completes its development on one plant or clump of plants, unless it succumbs to any one of a number of parasites or predators that prey on eggs, larvae or pupae.

Butterflies that do survive must then be able to obtain nectar from the available sources—plants their species may never have encountered in its evolutionary history. They show great flexibility: At least some butterflies can learn how to extract nectar from a wide variety of flowers, but there are always constraints imposed by flower shape, size and nectar quality. Finally, ever-present predators—birds, spiders and insects—are watching the butterflies' every move.

Given these challenges facing butterflies, we can glean a basic principle of butterfly gardening: Make things easy for butterflies as well as for yourself. Begin by grouping diverse clumps of attractive plants together in a sheltered, sunny spot. Leave some weedy patches and long grass nearby for egg-laying. Limit pesticide use. Don't worry about voracious caterpillars destroying your prized plants; they probably won't like them anyway and even if they do, their own enemies will limit their numbers far better than you can. But the most important principle may be to follow Christy's example by watching butterflies in any nearby open place, noting the flowers they visit. Grow these same plants in your own garden and you can bring to it the tranquility and peace butterflies impart in their lazy-looking flight.

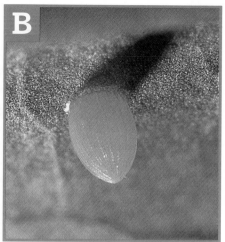

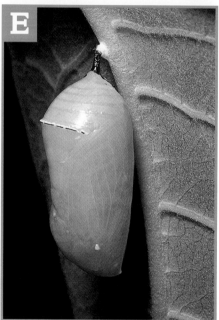

THE LIFE CYCLE OF A BUTTERFLY

A and **B**: After finding a suitable milkweed plant to provide larval food, the female Monarch lays her eggs, one at a time. **C**: The larva, or caterpillar, emerges and begins its mission of eating, growing and molting. **D** and **E**: When the caterpillar is fully grown in about 15 days, it begins its transformation

into a chrysalis, its pupal case. **F** : After two weeks, the wings are visible. **G** and **H** : The pupal case splits and the adult butterfly quickly emerges. The butterfly pumps a fluid from its body to its wings, which begin to stretch out.

DESIGNING GARDENS FOR BUTTERFLIES

BY ALICE YARBOROUGH

GARDENING FOR BUTTERFLIES is a suspenseful art, a bit like holding a picnic and wondering if your invited guests will show up. Butterflies are choosy insects. Any gardener can have aphids, but Red Admirals, Painted Ladies and Tiger Swallowtails insist that certain conditions be met.

Ample sunshine is the foremost consideration. Butterflies avoid shady areas. Ideally, your garden should have a southern exposure. Butterflies use early morning sunlight for basking on sun-warmed rocks, bricks or gravel paths. As morning temperatures rise, they begin visiting their favorite nectar flowers, but always in sunlit areas of the garden.

They prefer gardens that are sheltered from prevailing winds. If yours is not, consider planting a windscreen of lilac, mock orange, butterfly bush or viburnum—all shrubs whose flowers are rich in nectar.

A butterfly garden's style is not as important as its content. It should offer nectar flowers throughout the growing season. Luckily, many of our most loved annuals and perennials are top-notch nectar sources. While native American species play an important role as host plants for hungry butterfly caterpillars, most adult butterflies have cosmopolitan tastes, supping as readily on the nectar-filled flowers of *Hylotelephium spectabile,* a Chinese native, as they do on our own native bee balm, *Monarda didyma.*

Butterflies seem especially attracted to gardens boasting generous patches of a given nectar flower. If you plant red valerian, *Centranthus ruber,* don't settle for one or two specimens. Try growing three or more patches of this especially popular nectar flower, and watch the swallowtails drift from clump to clump.

Using the plant encyclopedia in this handbook, you may want to start from scratch and populate an entire garden solely with nectar plants. Most readers, however, will wish to enhance an existing garden with the addition of butterfly-attracting flowers and shrubs. Remember that a given flower that attracts butterflies in one area may not necessarily prove a favorite with differing species of butterflies elsewhere in the country. For example, butterfly weed, *Asclepias tuberosa,* although mobbed by butterflies in many sections of the U.S., is routinely ignored by those cruising my Pacific Northwest garden. Plants listed in the encyclopedia will attract butterflies in a wide range of locales. Experiment and learn which flowers your local butterflies prefer.

Because I love old-fashioned cottage gardens, my own butterfly garden is

Left: Alice Yarborough's Pacific Northwest butterfly garden is filled with informal groups of plants of many heights, in the old-fashioned cottage-garden style.

In late August, the garden features generous patches of nectar plants, including low growers spilling onto gravel paths.

filled with informal groups of plants of varied heights, including many low growers spilling forth onto the garden's gravel paths.

Grape hyacinths, pulmonaria, rock cress, azaleas, lilacs, wallflowers and pinks furnish nectar in early and mid spring. From late spring on through autumn, an abundance of excellent butterfly plants comes into bloom. *Primula vialii,* the June-blooming orchid primrose, is thickly interplanted with tall forget-me-nots. I use perennial alpine pinks, biennial sweet William and self-sowing annual candytuft to edge beds of red valerian and June-blooming yarrows such as pale yellow *Achillea* 'Taygetea' and *Achillea* 'Moonshine'. Tall perennial phlox and purple coneflowers are planted behind the red valerian to provide color and nectar in July and August.

Dominating one end of the garden, Joe-pye weed waves its butterfly-laden flowerheads on high for weeks in late summer. Planted in front of it, and sharing its bloom period, are patches of red monarda and the tall hybrid yarrow, 'Coronation Gold'. A large drift of purple-flowered anise hyssop, *Agastache foeniculum,* completes the picture. Although the garden hosts a considerable variety of nectar flowers, when anise hyssop and Joe-pye weed are in bloom butterflies concentrate on them—much as they mobbed other favorites earlier in the summer. Edging this bed are clumps of golden marjoram, oregano, rosy-flowered *Hylotelephium spectabile* 'Carmen' and the little Mexican daisy *Erigeron karvinskianus*—all excellent nectar plants.

In September and October, purple hardy asters, backed with golden heleniums and Taiyo sunflowers, create a dazzling picture. In my garden, original species asters attract far more bees and butterflies than do the modern hybrids.

Gardeners in arid sections of the country will find many butterfly flowers that are drought tolerant. Yarrow, lantana, verbena, coreopsis, lavender, butterfly weed, sedum, erigeron, hardy asters and centranthus all thrive on dry, sunny sites.

If your garden has a low, dampish area with indifferent drainage, plant moisture lovers like the rosy-flowered swamp milkweed (*Asclepias incarnata*), Joe-pye weed, forget-me-nots, monardas and meadow sweet (*Filipendula palmata*). Create a shallow puddle to attract swallowtails, blues, sulfurs and other butterflies that enjoy drinking at mud puddles. (They do so to obtain needed salts in their diet.) A sprinkling of table salt and the addition of some manure will increase the puddle's appeal for butterflies. Since salt harms plants, however, use a plastic liner or locate the

10 GUIDELINES FOR BUTTERFLY GARDENING

1.
Watch butterflies in nearby areas to see which flowers they prefer.

2
Grow these plants and ones recommended in this book.

3
Position plants in a sunny place, sheltered from wind.

4
Grow large clumps of the most favored species.

5
Try to maintain diversity in height, color and blooming periods.

6
Avoid or limit your use of pesticides.

7
Provide a mud puddle in a sunny spot.

8
Grow larval plants for butterflies that appear in your garden.

9
Try some plants in containers for increased flexibility.

10
Leave some undisturbed corners for weedy larval and nectar plants.

A butterfly garden doesn't have to be large to be effective. Here, nectar plants line a walkway.

puddle outside your flower border.

A butterfly gardener's bonus is that many nectar flowers are also popular with hummingbirds, bees and nocturnal hawk moths, such as the beautiful White-lined Sphinx.

Although many butterfly caterpillars subsist on leaves of native weeds and trees, you may discover certain ones within your flower garden as well. West Coast Ladies sometimes lay eggs on the leaves of ornamental mallows. Painted Ladies, which instinctively lay their eggs on thistle plants, also find an acceptable substitute in the hairy leaves of borage. Spying dozens of Painted Lady caterpillars on your borage plants does not mean the end result will be a crowd of butterflies emerging from their chrysalises in your garden. Alas! Such collections of juicy caterpillar morsels are handy food marts for wasps and hungry birds. Lucky is the caterpillar who survives to become a butterfly.

Don't fret too much about butterfly larvae chewing your prized plants to bits. Natural predators usually keep caterpillar populations under control. Also, the larvae of many butterfly species feed only on certain native plants and trees. Butterfly gardeners should not use insecticides and herbicides. Chemical warfare kills indiscriminately: Butterflies, their larvae and their natural predators are all destroyed. Organic gardeners tolerate a chewed leaf or blossom and handpick voracious insects or knock them off plants with water from the hose. You can also move offending butterfly caterpillars to other acceptable host plants nearby. I have transferred West Coast Lady larvae from ornamental mallow leaves to those of *Malva neglecta,* a common ground-hugging weed found in many gardens. Mostly, however, I welcome the occasional presence of butterfly caterpillars in my garden, sometimes carrying one indoors along with a spray of its food plant so that I can observe the miracle of metamorphosis.

Try keeping a brief journal of your butterfly-watching experiences. Buy a good field guide to help you identify your butterfly visitors as well as their eggs and caterpillars. Butterfly gardening can be a lifelong adventure that becomes more exciting as your knowledge grows.

ENCYCLOPEDIA

of
Butterflies

This encyclopedia includes some of the most commonly found U.S. butterfly species. They were chosen because of their wide distribution and to illustrate the major groups of butterflies encountered in gardens. Since the most common butterfly in your garden may not be listed here, consult one of the field guides on page 103 for help in identification. Each entry lists plants preferred by larvae and nectar sources favored by adults. For detailed descriptions of these plants, consult the Encyclopedia of Butterfly Plants beginning on page 36. For further information on other plant species used in your area, contact local natural history societies or your state non-game or urban wildlife departments.

GIANT SWALLOWTAIL

Swallowtails are large, showy butterflies with projections from the hind-wings resembling the tails of swallows. Their high, graceful flight may take them above the trees, but they readily descend to the garden to feed. The larvae of many species look like bird droppings and emit a foul defensive odor when touched.

RANGE: Throughout the eastern United States

HABITATS: Margins of hardwood forests, in citrus groves and around cultivated flowers in urban areas

LARVAL PLANTS: Citrus, torchwood, hop-tree, rue, prickly-ash, Hercules' club

NECTAR PLANTS: Lantana, butterfly bush, goldenrod, purple coneflower, Joe-pye weed, blanketflower, phlox, citrus, dame's rocket, bougainvillea, scarlet sage, golden dewdrop, lilac, milkweed, papaya, azalea, honeysuckle, pentas

ACTUAL WINGSPAN: 5.4"

EASTERN TIGER SWALLOWTAIL

F emale Tiger Swallowtails occur in two color forms, the tiger form or a smaller, darker form that resembles the Pipevine Swallowtail, a southern butterfly containing foul-tasting chemicals from its larval host plant. The dark form is more common in areas where there are more Pipevine Swallowtails.

RANGE: United States east of the Rockies, central Alaska and Canada

HABITATS: Woodlands, orchards, gardens and along rivers and roads

LARVAL PLANTS: Cherry, tulip tree, aspen, birch, lilac, hornbeam, willow, ash, sweet-bay, hop tree, spicebush

NECTAR PLANTS: Lilac, butterfly bush, thistle, ironweed, bee balm, honeysuckle, phlox, milkweed, buttonbush, lantana, hibiscus, sweet pepperbush, Hercules' club, figwort

SIMILAR SPECIES: The Western Tiger (*P. rutulus*), found west of the Rockies, is similar in appearance, but the ranges of the two species do not overlap. Nectar plants for the Western Tiger include hibiscus, red valerian and coastal buckwheat.

ACTUAL WINGSPAN: 4.3"

17

CABBAGE WHITE

ntroduced to Canada from Europe in the 19th century, the Cabbage White has become one of the most widespread butterflies in America. It adapts readily to new situations; for instance, it learns how to find nectar within flowers and can even learn to use the holes made by nectar-robbing bees to extract nectar from long-tubed flowers.

RANGE: Most of North America

HABITATS: Nearly every open habitat if mustards grow nearby; open woods, forest edges, agricultural fields, plains, gardens

LARVAL PLANTS: Members of the mustard family, including cabbage, winter cress, wallflower, nasturtium and peppergrass, as well as members of the caper family, such as cleome or spider flower

NECTAR PLANTS: Mints, asters, dandelion, clovers, dogbane, selfheal, bee balm, monkey flower, deerweed, passion flower, wallflower, pincushion flower, cinquefoil, lantana, cherry pie, dame's rocket and other mustards

SIMILAR SPECIES: The Checkered White (*Pontia protodice*) has checkered black markings on the wing.

ACTUAL WINGSPAN: 2.15"

CLOUDED SULPHUR

Sulphurs are a group of yellow, medium-sized butterflies—bright additions to the garden. Males congregate at mud puddles to collect salts and other nutrients. Females distinguish between similar males of different species by the differing amounts of ultraviolet reflection from the wings.

RANGE: Throughout much of the United States, although rare in the Southeast

HABITATS: Open areas, meadows, roadsides and agricultural fields, especially alfalfa fields

LARVAL PLANTS: Many members of the legume family, including alfalfa, white sweet clover, clovers, vetch, trefoil

NECTAR PLANTS: Clover, tithonia, phlox, milkweed, goldenrod, dandelion, asters, knapweed, dogbane, winter cress, dame's rocket, pincushion flower, globe thistle, marigold, pentas, scarlet sage, leadplant, leadwort, gayfeather, sedum, zinnia

SIMILAR SPECIES: The Orange Sulphur (*C. eurytheme*) male is similar to the Clouded male in pattern, but is more orange in color. The Cloudless Sulphur (*Phoebis sennae*) lacks the black border on the upper wing.

ACTUAL WINGSPAN: 2.15"

GRAY HAIRSTREAK

Brown or gray butterflies with distinctive markings, hairstreaks have projections on the rear of the hindwing resembling antennae. Coupled with eye-like markings, these pseudo-antennae apparently fool predators into attacking the rear, giving the butterfly a chance to escape. The Gray Hairstreak is one of the most common hairstreaks found in gardens, but it is tiny and camouflaged, presenting an exciting challenge to the butterfly gardener.

RANGE: Entire United States

HABITATS: Weedy disturbed areas, fields, roadsides, chaparral, open forests

LARVAL PLANTS: Plants of many families, including members of the pea and mallow families, such as clover, vetch, beans, tick-trefoil, bush clover, mallow, hollyhocks, rose of Sharon and hibiscus

NECTAR PLANTS: Milkweed, dogbane, mint, goldenrod, sedum, plumbago, Queen Anne's lace and many members of the pea family, including white sweet clover, yellow sweet clover, tick-trefoil, everlasting pea

ACTUAL WINGSPAN: 1.5"

EASTERN TAILED BLUE

Blues are small but beautiful butterflies—delightful additions to gardens. The iridescent flash of a patrolling male is one of the first signs of butterfly activity in the spring.

RANGE: Throughout the United States, but rare or absent in much of the South and limited to wetlands or disturbed areas in the West

HABITATS: Old fields, vacant lots, flower gardens, meadows, dunes and roadsides

LARVAL PLANTS: Beggar's-ticks, sweet clovers, vetches, bush clover and alfalfa

NECTAR PLANTS: Milkweed, dogbane, clover, cinquefoil, wild strawberry, fleabane, coreopsis, zinnia, wild geranium

SIMILAR SPECIES: The Western Tailed Blue (*Everes amyntula*) is closely related, but is not likely to be found in gardens. In the West, the Acmon Blue (*Plebejus acmon*) is most likely to be found in gardens.

ACTUAL WINGSPAN: 1.1"

21

SPRING AZURE

Caterpillars of many blues are tended by ants; the caterpillars secrete "honeydew" and a protein-rich substance to feed ants, which in turn protect the caterpillars by repelling parasites and predators.

RANGE: Throughout the United States except parts of Texas, Louisiana and Florida

HABITATS: Open woodlands, fields, roadsides and brushy areas

LARVAL PLANTS: The flowers and developing seeds of many trees and shrubs, including dogwood, blueberry, viburnum, cherry, sumac, ceanothus and privet

NECTAR PLANTS: Dogwood, holly, blackberry, milkweed, spicebush, forget-me-not, dandelion, privet, lilac, ceanothus, rock cress, cherry, cotoneaster, violet, coreopsis, leadwort, coastal buckwheat

SIMILAR SPECIES: The Silvery Blue (*Glaucopsyche lygdamus*) is similar to the Spring Azure.

ACTUAL WINGSPAN: 1.15"

22

GULF FRITILLARY

This spectacular butterfly is not a true fritillary, but a member of a largely tropical family known as the longwings. It adapts easily to city life.

RANGE: Southern United States, but adults may migrate northward through the Plains states in the summer

HABITATS: Forest margins, open fields, scrub and urban areas

LARVAL PLANTS: Passionflower

NECTAR PLANTS: Golden dewdrop, firebush, blazing star, pentas, scarlet sage, lantana, daisy, thistle, passion flower, hibiscus, impatiens

ACTUAL WINGSPAN: 2.9"

23

GREAT SPANGLED FRITILLARY

T his is a lovely butterfly with a slow, relaxed flight. It is known for its lengthy nectaring sessions on flowers, especially thistle.

RANGE: Throughout the United States except Florida

HABITATS: Open woodlands, moist areas, wet meadows

LARVAL PLANTS: Violets

NECTAR PLANTS: Thistle, coneflower, Joe-pye weed, ironweed, black-eyed Susan, blanketflower, New Jersey tea, dogbane, loosestrife, milkweed, verbena, mountain laurel, bee balm, red clover, globe thistle, red valerian, lantana, leadplant, catmint, pentas, scarlet sage, buttonbush; also rotting fruit and dung

SIMILAR SPECIES: Many species of fritillaries are similar in appearance and difficult to distinguish; this is the largest and is widely found.

ACTUAL WINGSPAN: 3.1"

24

PEARL CRESCENT

T he most common eastern butterfly, the Pearl Crescent is inquisitive, darting out after passing objects. The males patrol areas searching for females and visit moist ground for nutrients. Eggs are laid in clusters, and the larvae feed communally.

RANGE: Almost the entire United States, but abundant in the East and limited in most of the West

HABITATS: Flower gardens, fields, meadows, vacant lots, open wetlands, roadsides

LARVAL PLANTS: Asters, including Michaelmas daisy

NECTAR PLANTS: Asters, fleabane, daisy, black-eyed Susan, dogbane, milkweed, frogfruit, white clover, geranium, wallflower, mint, zinnia, coreopsis, cherry pie

SIMILAR SPECIES: The closely related Northern Crescent (*Phyciodes selenis*) is found in the North and in western mountains. The Mylitta Crescent (*Phyciodes mylitta*) or Field Crescent (*Phyciodes campestris*) might be found in western gardens.

ACTUAL WINGSPAN: 1.5"

QUESTION MARK

This butterfly belongs to the group known as anglewings ("polygonia" means "many angles"). When butterflies of this group close their wings, the camouflaged underside blends perfectly with tree bark. Males are often found on tree trunks or limbs, especially if sap is flowing from a wound.

RANGE: East of the Rockies from Florida to Canada

HABITATS: Wooded areas, open sunny areas near forests, roads and streamsides

LARVAL PLANTS: Nettle, elm, hackberry, hops, false nettle

NECTAR PLANTS: Prefers rotting fruit, sapflows, dung and carrion, but will come to asters, milkweed, sweet pepperbush, zinnia

SIMILAR SPECIES: The Question Mark is distinguished from the Eastern Comma (*Polygonia comma*) and other similar butterflies by a silver mark on the underside of its wings.

ACTUAL WINGSPAN: 2.9"

MOURNING CLOAK

An elegant butterfly, the Mourning Cloak hibernates as an adult in protected places such as hollow logs or outbuildings. It is seen sporadically throughout the winter and early spring. Males choose areas as large as 300 square yards to patrol for females; they appear to defend these areas, chasing away other males and even other insects and birds.

RANGE: Throughout the United States; common in the North and absent or rare in the South

HABITATS: Woodlands, swamps, streamsides, suburban areas

LARVAL PLANTS: Willows, cottonwoods, aspen, elms, birches and hackberry

NECTAR PLANTS: Sap flows at trees; butterfly bush, New Jersey tea, almond, rabbitbrush, milkweed, dogbane, mountain andromeda, moss pink, rock cress, zinnia, red valerian

ACTUAL WINGSPAN: 2.9"

MILBERT'S TORTOISESHELL

The group of butterflies called tortoiseshells have jagged wing margins and camouflaged undersides of both fore- and hindwings. Milbert's Tortoiseshell comes readily to gardens, although like its relatives, it prefers sap flows and rotting fruit. Since it overwinters in the adult stage, it may be seen on a warm day in midwinter, finally emerging for good in early spring, faded and tattered. Wood and brush piles and outbuildings provide overwintering sites.

RANGE: Northern United States; occasionally strays south

HABITATS: Moist pastures and fields near woodlands, near streams in western mountains

LARVAL PLANTS: Nettles

NECTAR PLANTS: Thistle, sneezeweed, goldenrod, aster, marigold, daisy, wallflower, ageratum, butterfly bush, lilac, sedum, rock cress, bee balm, Joe-pye weed, zinnia, red valerian, anise hyssop; also rotting fruit and sap flows

ACTUAL WINGSPAN: 2.2"

PAINTED LADY

This pretty butterfly is the most widely distributed butterfly in the world and is attracted to gardens. It is known for its periodic migrations.

RANGE: Entire United States, but not every year

HABITATS: Old fields, vacant lots, gardens, meadows, mountains, deserts

LARVAL PLANTS: More than 100 different plants, including thistle, knapweed, groundsel, sunflower, pearly everlasting, wormwood, hollyhock, common mallow

NECTAR PLANTS: Thistle, Joe-pye weed, gayfeather, aster, zinnia, tithonia, goldenrod, butterfly bush, buttonbush, bee balm, sedum, privet, wallflower, globe thistle, red valerian, anise hyssop, pincushion flower, phlox, monkey flower, deerweed, leadplant, passion flower, coastal buckwheat, leadwort

SIMILAR SPECIES: Often confused with the American Lady (*Vanessa virginiensis*) and West Coast Lady (*Vanessa annabella*), it is distinguished by the size, number and clarity of the eyespots on the hindwing.

ACTUAL WINGSPAN: 2.6"

RED ADMIRAL

A favorite of many gardeners, this butterfly may actually help to control nettles. Like many butterflies, it is fond of salt and may alight on the exposed skin of the gardener. Males establish a new territory every afternoon, perching in bright spots and flying after anything that enters it.

RANGE: Throughout the United States

HABITATS: A wide range, from the edge of tundra to the subtropical forests of the Florida Keys, including gardens and parks

LARVAL PLANTS: Members of the nettle family, including burning nettle, false nettle, and pellitory; occasionally hops

NECTAR PLANTS: Tree sap, juice from fallen fruit; butterfly bush, milkweed, sedum, wallflower, fireweed, mint, sweet pepperbush, hebe, aster, Spanish needle, coreopsis, blanketflower, lantana, leadplant, catmint, phlox, anise hyssop, pincushion flower, leadwort

ACTUAL WINGSPAN: 2.6"

COMMON BUCKEYE

The Buckeye is satisfying for the beginner since it's easily identified. It likes to bask on bare ground and visit mud puddles. The males appear to be territorial, perching and patroling for females.

RANGE: Spreads from the South throughout most of the United States as summer progresses

HABITATS: Open areas, coastlines, fields, meadows, railroad tracks

LARVAL PLANTS: Plantain, verbena, many members of the snapdragon family, including snapdragon, false foxglove, figwort, toadflax, monkey flower

NECTAR PLANTS: Milkweed, aster, coreopsis, chicory, knapweed, plantain, dogbane, butterfly bush, mints, buckwheat, globe thistle

ACTUAL WINGSPAN: 2.2"

VICEROY

The Viceroy belongs to a "mimicry ring" with the Monarch and Queen; the bright colors of this group are thought to serve as a warning to predators. (Some of the milkweed plants fed on by Monarch larvae are toxic to bird predators, so birds learn to avoid the Monarch. Both the Viceroy and the Queen resemble, or "mimic" the Monarch, and bird predators avoid them as well.)

RANGE: Almost throughout the United States, but absent from the Pacific coast and rare elsewhere in the arid West

HABITATS: Edges of woodlands, marshes, streamsides, meadows

LARVAL PLANTS: Willow, aspen, poplar, apple, plum, cherry

NECTAR PLANTS: Goldenrod, Joe-pye weed, thistle, milkweed, leadwort, catmint, phlox; also rotting fruit, sap, bird droppings or dung

SIMILAR SPECIES: Easily confused with the Monarch in most of its range and with the Queen (*Danaus gilippus*) in the deep South and Southwest.

ACTUAL WINGSPAN: 3.25"

MONARCH

Perhaps the best known and most popular of all butterflies, the Monarch is also the most migratory.

RANGE: Throughout the United States

HABITATS: Open areas, including urban areas

LARVAL PLANTS: Various members of the milkweed family

NECTAR PLANTS: Milkweed, butterfly bush, aster, thistle, mistflower, goldenrod, tithonia, Joe-pye weed, blanketflower, gayfeather, cosmos, lantana, scarlet sage, abelia, lilac, lantana, mallow, mint, sedum, dogbane, firebush, pentas, golden dewdrop, zinnia

SIMILAR SPECIES: The Queen (*Danaus gilippus*) and Viceroy (*Limenitis archippus*) both mimic the Monarch.

ACTUAL WINGSPAN: 4.3"

SILVER-SPOTTED SKIPPER

S kippers are a large group falling between butterflies and moths. They are stout-bodied day fliers that hold their forewings and hindwings at different angles at rest (although the wingspan is illustrated below, you'll never see a live Skipper with its wings spread and flattened out). The Silver-spotted Skipper is especially noticeable because of its large silver spots, probably used to advertise its presence to other members of the same species.

RANGE: Throughout the United States, but absent in much of the arid West and mountainous regions

HABITATS: Gardens, woodland openings, streamsides, roadsides

LARVAL PLANTS: Locust, wisteria, wild licorice, beggar's-ticks, hog peanut

NECTAR PLANTS: Milkweed, dogbane, buttonbush, Hercules' club, honeysuckle, selfheal, viper's bugloss, gayfeather, globe thistle, pentas, golden dewdrop, zinnia, sweet pepperbush, leadplant, purple coneflower, Joe-pye weed, blanketflower

SIMILAR SPECIES: The smaller Hoary Edge (*Achalarus lyciades*), although not closely related, somewhat resembles the Silver-spotted Skipper and is found throughout the eastern United States.

ACTUAL WINGSPAN: 1.5"

FIERY SKIPPER

The Fiery Skipper is readily attracted to gardens, where it adds a warm flash of color, especially as males fly out from their perches searching for females. Caterpillars escape the lawn mower in shelters at the base of grass stems. (Note: although the Fiery Skipper's wingspan is illustrated below, you'll never see it with its wings spread and flattened out.)

RANGE: Eastern and southwestern United States

HABITATS: Fields, roadsides, levees, second-growth scrub, lawns, grasslands

LARVAL PLANTS: Weedy grasses, including bentgrass, crabgrass, Bermudagrass, St. Augustinegrass, sugar cane

NECTAR PLANTS: Abelia, sweet pepperbush, statice, sneezeweed, beggar's-ticks, knapweed, lantana, milkweed, aster, thistle, ironweed, purple coneflower, buckwheat, leadplant, zinnia, sedum, verbena

SIMILAR SPECIES: Whirlabout (*Polites vibex*) has large, smudged brown or black spots as opposed to the numerous, smaller spots on the Fiery Skipper.

ACTUAL WINGSPAN: 1.0"

of
Butterfly Plants

This plant encyclopedia includes scores of widely grown and widely available nectar plants for butterflies. Just one species for each genus is featured, but additional related species and cultivars are given where appropriate. Not all the butterflies using each plant are listed. In addition to the featured plants, most herbs, if left to flower, are very attractive to most butterflies—particularly blues, whites, sulphurs, hairstreaks, nymphalids and skippers. Grow them in large clumps with other nectar plants.

To find your hardiness zone, check the map on page 106; if you live in the West, consult the detailed maps in SUNSET WESTERN GARDEN BOOK, published by the editors of Sunset Books and SUNSET magazine.

NATIVE HABITAT: Hybrid
GROWTH TYPE: Broadleaved shrub, evergreen in South, deciduous in North
HARDINESS ZONE: USDA 6 to 10, Sunset 5 to 24
FLOWER COLOR: White to pale pink
HEIGHT: Up to 8'
BLOOMING PERIOD: June until frost
HOW TO GROW: Prefers full sun protected from wind in rich, moist, well-drained soil, but will tolerate shade and drought. Winter dieback may occur in northern areas, but new growth will come back quickly. Bronze or purplish fall foliage. Best as an untrimmed specimen plant. Hardy and fast growing with no significant disease or insect problems.

BUTTERFLIES ATTRACTED: Almost all the butterflies flying during its several-month blooming period, especially swallowtails.

CULTIVARS AND RELATED SPECIES: 'Edward Goucher'—Lower growing; lilac-pink; more finely textured foliage. 'Prostrata' and 'Sherwoodii'—Excellent large-scale ground and bank covers.

YARROW

NATIVE HABITAT: Hybrid

GROWTH TYPE: Herbaceous perennial

HARDINESS ZONE: USDA 3 to 9, Sunset all zones

FLOWER COLOR: Lemon-yellow

HEIGHT: 3'

BLOOMING PERIOD: Several weeks beginning in midsummer

HOW TO GROW: Full sun in either average or poor well-drained soil. Avoid high-nitrogen fertilizers. Tolerates drought well. Divide in the spring every three or four years.

BUTTERFLIES ATTRACTED: Various, including coppers, hairstreaks, skippers, Mylitta Crescent.

CULTIVARS AND RELATED SPECIES:
A. 'Taygetea'—Primrose-yellow flowers in flat clusters above feathery grayish foliage; 18 to 24" tall.

A. 'Moonshine'—Flowers are smaller and paler than 'Coronation Gold'; foliage is grayer. Less erect, 24 to 30" tall.

A. filipendulina 'Gold Plate', Fernleaf yarrow—Rich yellow flowers on 5' stalks, blooming mid to late summer.

A. millefolium, Common yarrow—White or rose flowerheads over feathery dark green foliage, 12 to 24" tall. Somewhat aggressive; hybrid forms are less aggressive.

ANISE HYSSOP

NATIVE HABITAT: North central North America; meadows and woodlands

GROWTH TYPE: Herbaceous perennial

HARDINESS ZONE: USDA 3, Sunset 1 to 9, 14 to 21

FLOWER COLOR: Bluish-purple

HEIGHT: 4 to 5'

BLOOMING PERIOD: Midsummer to early autumn

HOW TO GROW: Full sun in moist, well-drained soil. Can be grown from seed sown indoors in March to produce bushy, flower-laden plants by late July. Cut top growth back to ground in late fall. Seed heads remain decorative after flowering ceases.

BUTTERFLIES ATTRACTED: A wide variety, including Red Admiral, Mylitta Crescent, Painted Lady, Milbert's Tortoiseshell, sulphurs.

CULTIVARS AND RELATED SPECIES:

A. urticifolia—Less showy, rosy flower spikes, 3 to 4' tall.

A. cana, Hummingbird mint—New Mexico native; dark pink; 3' tall.

MIMOSA · SILK TREE · POWDERPUFF-TREE

NATIVE HABITAT: Iran to China; has naturalized on roadsides and in thickets and forest edges in parts of Virginia, Kentucky and Indiana

GROWTH TYPE: Deciduous tree

HARDINESS ZONE: USDA 6 to 10, Sunset 2 to 23

FLOWER COLOR: Pale pink to dark rose

HEIGHT: 15 to 25'

BLOOMING PERIOD: April through August

HOW TO GROW: Best in sun where summers are hot. Grows in almost any well-drained soil, but needs some watering. Tolerates air pollution well. Fast-growing and can be brittle. Will form an almost solid canopy of feathery pink blossoms. Branches are best left untrimmed to avoid pest damage. The fern-like leaves close at night.

BUTTERFLIES ATTRACTED: A wide variety, especially sulphurs and swallowtails.

CULTIVARS AND RELATED SPECIES: 'Rosea'—A smaller tree with deeper pink flowers.
'Charlotte'—Blight resistant.
'Tryon'—Blight resistant.

NATIVE HABITAT: Central North America; grasslands

GROWTH TYPE: Shrub in warmer climates, herbaceous perennial elsewhere

HARDINESS ZONE: USDA 4 to 9, Sunset 1 to 9, 14 to 20

FLOWER COLOR: Indigo blue

HEIGHT: 4'

BLOOMING PERIOD: Mid to late summer for three weeks

HOW TO GROW: Insists on full sun, but is quite tolerant of varying soil types, from clay to sand. Very drought tolerant once established. Lovely, fine-textured gray-green pinnate foliage sets off the showy flower spikes. Combine with butterfly weed for midsummer beauty.

BUTTERFLIES ATTRACTED: Painted Lady, Red Admiral, fritillaries, sulphurs, blues, skippers.

CULTIVARS AND RELATED SPECIES: *A. fruticosa*—A large, coarse shrub best left for naturalizing.

A. nana—A rare dwarf form to 1'. Slightly more lavender, fragrant flowers.

SPREADING DOGBANE

NATIVE HABITAT: Eastern North America, Texas and Arizona; upland woods, fields
GROWTH TYPE: Herbaceous perennial
HARDINESS ZONE: USDA 3 to 9, Sunset 1 to 9, 14 to 21

FLOWER COLOR: Pale pink or white
HEIGHT: 1 to 4'
BLOOMING PERIOD: Each plant blooms for a short period (about two weeks), any time from June to August, depending on conditions.
HOW TO GROW: Full sun. Can be aggressive; plant away from formal areas of the garden.
BUTTERFLIES ATTRACTED: A wide variety, including swallowtails, sulphurs, coppers, hairstreaks, blues, nymphalids, Monarch, skippers; occasionally used as a host plant by the Monarch.

AQUILEGIA FORMOSA

WESTERN COLUMBINE

NATIVE HABITAT: Utah and California to Alaska; mountain woodland clearings
GROWTH TYPE: Herbaceous perennial
HARDINESS ZONE: USDA 3 to 8, Sunset all zones
FLOWER COLOR: Red and yellow
HEIGHT: 1-1/2 to 3'
BLOOMING PERIOD: Spring, early summer
HOW TO GROW: Filtered to full sun. Trim old stems after flowering. New plants may be needed every few years.
BUTTERFLIES ATTRACTED: Various, including swallowtails and fritillaries.

DEVIL'S WALKING STICK • HERCULES' CLUB

NATIVE HABITAT: Western New York to Iowa, south to Florida; upland woods, clearings

GROWTH TYPE: Shrub

HARDINESS ZONE: USDA 4 to 9, Sunset 2 to 24

FLOWER COLOR: White

HEIGHT: 8 to 12'

BLOOMING PERIOD: Late July to August

HOW TO GROW: Partial shade to full sun in the poorest soils. It suckers readily and can be divided if it becomes too aggressive.

BUTTERFLIES ATTRACTED: A wide variety, including Eastern Tiger Swallowtail, Spicebush Swallowtail, Black Swallowtail, Silver-spotted Skipper, Red-banded Hairstreak.

BUTTERFLY WEED

NATIVE HABITAT: Central and eastern North America; fields, dry soil
GROWTH TYPE: Herbaceous perennial
HARDINESS ZONE: USDA 3 to 10, Sunset all zones
FLOWER COLOR: Brilliant orange
HEIGHT: 2 to 3'
BLOOMING PERIOD: June to September
HOW TO GROW: Full sun, good drainage and little water. Susceptible to aphids. Remove dead flowers to extend bloom.

BUTTERFLIES ATTRACTED: One of the best butterfly plants, attracting a very wide variety of butterflies; a larval host plant of the Monarch.
CULTIVARS AND RELATED SPECIES:
A. syriaca, Common milkweed—Pink-white flowers.
A. incarnata, Swamp milkweed—Bright pink flowers.
A. curassavica, Scarlet milkweed—Tropical plant with brilliant red and yellow flowers, very attractive to butterflies. Care should be taken in warmer areas to avoid self-seeding.

NEW ENGLAND ASTER

NATIVE HABITAT: New England to Alabama, westward to North Dakota and Wyoming; damp thickets, wet meadows, margins of marshes

GROWTH TYPE: Herbaceous perennial

HARDINESS ZONE: USDA 3 to 9, Sunset all zones

FLOWER COLOR: Violet-purple

HEIGHT: 2 to 8'

BLOOMING PERIOD: Mid-August through October

HOW TO GROW: Full sun in moist soil that is not too rich. To avoid staking and for a bushier plant, prune growing tips in early summer. Can be aggressive. For an attractive low-maintenance planting, group this species in a meadow with goldenrods, native grasses and other asters. Since it is late blooming, it is an excellent nectar source for fall migrants.

BUTTERFLIES ATTRACTED: A wide variety, including Monarch, Pearl Crescent, Painted Lady, American Lady, Cloudless Sulphur, skippers, hairstreaks.

CULTIVARS AND RELATED SPECIES: 'Purple Dome'—Short, bushy habit. 'Alma Potschke'—Deep pink flowers.

45

BUTTERFLY BUSH

NATIVE HABITAT: Northwest China; dry lowland habitats

GROWTH TYPE: Shrub

HARDINESS ZONE: USDA 5 to 10, Sunset all zones

FLOWER COLOR: Lavender, pink, white, purple, magenta

HEIGHT: Up to 10 to 12'

BLOOMING PERIOD: Late July to frost

HOW TO GROW: Full sun in well-drained soil. Protect from midday sun in deep South. In cold climates soft wood will die back, but roots are hardy. Cut all branches back, since the best flowers bloom on new growth.

BUTTERFLIES ATTRACTED: A wide variety, including Monarch, swallowtails, nymphalids and skippers; may be the best all-around butterfly-attracting plant.

CULTIVARS AND RELATED SPECIES: Many named varieties; the white-flowered butterfly bush may be most attractive to butterflies.

'Petite Plum'—Dwarf form.

B. alternifolia—Blooms in June on long, arching branches with silver leaves.

B. fallowiana 'Lochinch'—Grows to 5' tall; lavender flowers. Not completely hardy in Zone 5.

NATIVE HABITAT: Central Maine to western Ontario, south to Gulf; dry open woods and rocky banks
GROWTH TYPE: Shrub
HARDINESS ZONE: USDA 4 to 8, Sunset 4 to 7, 14 to 24
FLOWER COLOR: Creamy white
HEIGHT: 3 to 5'
BLOOMING PERIOD: Spring
HOW TO GROW: Sun in light, well-drained soil. Takes a few years to establish while putting down roots. Makes an excellent hedge. Watch for Japanese beetles.
BUTTERFLIES ATTRACTED: Spring butterflies, including Spring Azure.

RED VALERIAN • JUPITER'S BEARD

NATIVE HABITAT: Europe and North Africa; sunny, dry, waste places
GROWTH TYPE: Herbaceous perennial
HARDINESS ZONE: USDA 5 to 8, Sunset 7 to 9, 12 to 24
FLOWER COLOR: Rosy red
HEIGHT: 30"
BLOOMING PERIOD: Mid-May to late July
HOW TO GROW: Full sun, well-drained soil. Water occasionally; tolerates drought well. May be invasive; remove spent flowers to prevent self-sowing. Cut stalks back in late fall.
BUTTERFLIES ATTRACTED: Many species, including Mourning Cloak, Painted Lady, Western Tiger Swallowtail, Milbert's Tortoiseshell, Great Spangled Fritillary.
CULTIVARS AND RELATED SPECIES: 'Alba'—White-flowered; equally attractive to butterflies.

BUTTON-BUSH

NATIVE HABITAT: California to Mexico to Florida, north to New York and Canada; low moist areas, edges of marshes, river banks
GROWTH TYPE: Deciduous multi-trunked large shrub or small tree
HARDINESS ZONE: USDA 5 to 10, Sunset 4 to 24
FLOWER COLOR: Creamy white to pink

HEIGHT: 3 to 5' (sometimes to 18')
BLOOMING PERIOD: June to September
HOW TO GROW: Sun to semi-shade. Does best in moist, sandy loam, but will grow in almost any soil. Can tolerate drier conditions in gardens than it finds in its native habitat, but will need supplemental water. Prune vigorously every two to three years to control spreading and to encourage flowering. Flowers are numerous and very fragrant; even the seed balls have a spicy aroma.
BUTTERFLIES ATTRACTED: One of the best native shrubs for almost all butterflies.

FALSE PLUMBAGO • LEADWORT

NATIVE HABITAT: Western China; alpine meadows
GROWTH TYPE: Herbaceous perennial
HARDINESS ZONE: USDA 4 to 8, Sunset 2 to 10, 14 to 24
FLOWER COLOR: Vivid gentian blue
HEIGHT: 1'
BLOOMING PERIOD: Six weeks in late summer and autumn

HOW TO GROW: Morning sun and some afternoon shade. Tolerates a range of soil types with average moisture. Makes a slow-growing groundcover, excellent as a companion to bulbs. Emerges late in the spring. The foliage turns brilliant red in the fall, stunning with the last of its sapphire-blue flowers.
BUTTERFLIES ATTRACTED: Painted Lady, Red Admiral, Viceroy, blues, sulphurs.
CULTIVARS AND RELATED SPECIES: *C. willmottianum*—Small shrub with similar characteristics.

TURTLEHEAD · SNAKE-HEAD · BALMONY

NATIVE HABITAT: Newfoundland to Ontario and Minnesota, south to Georgia, Alabama, Missouri; low moist areas, ditches, swamps, stream banks

GROWTH TYPE: Herbaceous perennial

HARDINESS ZONE: USDA 3 to 9, Sunset 1 to 24

FLOWER COLOR: White or pink-tinged on top

HEIGHT: 1 to 3'

BLOOMING PERIOD: Mid-August through September

HOW TO GROW: Semi-shade in rich, moist soil. Mulch with compost or rotted leaves. Clumps spread rapidly, and plant self-sows readily.

BUTTERFLIES ATTRACTED: Silver-spotted Skipper, Spicebush Swallowtail, Eastern Tiger Swallowtail. Turtlehead is the favored larval host plant of the

Chelone lyonii

Baltimore (*Euphydryas phaeton*), which is rare or threatened in several states.

CULTIVARS AND RELATED SPECIES:

C. lyonii—Rose-pink flowers.

C. obliqua—Rose-red flowers.

DESERT WILLOW

NATIVE HABITAT: Southwestern United States to Mexico; washes, the wettest areas in desert environments

GROWTH TYPE: Shrub or tree

HARDINESS ZONE: USDA 8, Sunset 11 to 13, 18 to 21

FLOWER COLOR: Pink, white, rose or lavender with purple markings

HEIGHT: To 20'

BLOOMING PERIOD: Spring and again in fall

HOW TO GROW: Full sun, prefers well-drained, limestone soil. Needs little water. Can be trained as a tree but severe pruning will encourage flowering.

BUTTERFLIES ATTRACTED: A wide variety of butterflies, including swallowtails.

RABBITBRUSH

NATIVE HABITAT: Western United States; dry stream beds

GROWTH TYPE: Shrub

HARDINESS ZONE: USDA 8 to 10, Sunset 8 to 9, 12 to 16, 18 to 23

FLOWER COLOR: Yellow

HEIGHT: 2 to 4'

BLOOMING PERIOD: August into October

HOW TO GROW: Full sun in almost any well-drained soil. Water sparingly—too much kills or produces floppy plants. Prune for maximum flower production and to control rangy appearance. Will not invade rangeland, but is avoided by cattle so spreads in over-grazed land.

BUTTERFLIES ATTRACTED: Many, including Monarch, whites, sulphurs, nymphalids, skippers.

CULTIVARS AND RELATED SPECIES: Cultivars varying in blooming time and height are available.

52

SWEET PEPPERBUSH • SUMMERSWEET

NATIVE HABITAT: Eastern North America; swamps, sandy soils
GROWTH TYPE: Deciduous shrub
HARDINESS ZONE: USDA 5 to 10, Sunset 2 to 6
FLOWER COLOR: White
HEIGHT: 10'
BLOOMING PERIOD: Late July to August
HOW TO GROW: Full sun, with protection in midday in South. Acid soil. Little care is needed except pruning in spring to desired height. Handsome late-flowering shrub with wonderful fragrance. The leaves turn brilliant yellow in the autumn and make a wonderful display.
BUTTERFLIES ATTRACTED: A wide variety, especially Silver-spotted Skipper and swallowtails.

LANCE-LEAVED COREOPSIS • TICKSEED

Coreopsis verticillata

NATIVE HABITAT: Southern New England and Michigan, south to Florida and Texas; fields and roadsides

GROWTH TYPE: Herbaceous perennial

HARDINESS ZONE: USDA 3 to 9, Sunset all zones

FLOWER COLOR: Golden yellow

HEIGHT: 1 to 3'

BLOOMING PERIOD: Late May through July

HOW TO GROW: Full sun in sandy, well-drained soil. Will tolerate dry soils and a wide range of soil pHs. Remove dead flowerheads to extend bloom. Long season.

BUTTERFLIES ATTRACTED: A wide variety, including Eastern Tailed Blue, Spring Azure, Pearl Crescent, Orange Sulphur, American Copper, Viceroy, Red Admiral.

CULTIVARS AND RELATED SPECIES: *C. verticillata*—Small golden yellow flowers from June to September. *C. rosea*—Pink flowers.

54

ALLWOOD'S ALPINE PINK

NATIVE HABITAT: Hybrid
GROWTH TYPE: Evergreen perennial
HARDINESS ZONE: USDA 3 to 10,
Sunset 1 to 11, 14 to 21
FLOWER COLOR: Pink single flowers,
many with contrasting red or maroon
eyes
HEIGHT: Low, spreading mat
BLOOMING PERIOD: May through June
HOW TO GROW: Sun, in lean, well-
drained, slightly alkaline soil. Requires
little water. Shearing the faded flowers
stimulates reblooming. The spreading
mat of blue-gray foliage is decorative
throughout the year.

BUTTERFLIES ATTRACTED: Numerous
species, including several species of
swallowtails, Clodius Parnassian, West
Coast Lady, Red Admiral, Mourning
Cloak.
CULTIVARS AND RELATED SPECIES:
'Spottii'—Compact, gray-green cush-
ion; fragrant white flowers laced with
ruby red.
D. barbatus, Sweet William—Sun and
lime lover. Old-fashioned taller varieties are spicily fragrant and loved by
butterflies. Not a true biennial, but
best handled as one for maximum
bloom.

Duranta erecta (D. repens)

GOLDEN DEWDROP · PIGEON BERRY

NATIVE HABITAT: West Indies to Brazil; forests, riversides
GROWTH TYPE: Large evergreen shrub
HARDINESS ZONE: USDA 9 to 10, Sunset 13, 16, 17, 21 to 24
FLOWER COLOR: Lilac, rarely white
HEIGHT: To 18'
BLOOMING PERIOD: All year
HOW TO GROW: Prefers sun, high heat, moist soil. Control by pruning and thinning. Very salt tolerant. Useful as a freestanding specimen or tall barrier hedge.

BUTTERFLIES ATTRACTED: Large sulphurs, swallowtails, fritillaries, skippers, Monarch.

Echinacea purpurea

PURPLE CONEFLOWER

NATIVE HABITAT: North American prairie
GROWTH TYPE: Herbaceous perennial
HARDINESS ZONE: USDA 3 to 9, Sunset all zones
FLOWER COLOR: Purple ray flowers
HEIGHT: 2 to 4'
BLOOMING PERIOD: June to October
HOW TO GROW: Full sun. Easy to grow with few problems. Deadheading encourages continuous flower production.
BUTTERFLIES ATTRACTED: Many, including Tiger Swallowtail, hairstreaks, skippers, Viceroy, Great Spangled Fritillary.
CULTIVARS AND RELATED SPECIES:

E. angustifolia—2' tall; rose-purple ray flowers.

E. pallida—3' tall; similar to above.

GLOBE THISTLE · RUSSIAN GLOBE THISTLE

NATIVE HABITAT: Eastern Europe and Russia; mountain riverbanks, streambanks, steppe meadows, disturbed sites, stony slopes, rarely broadleaved forests

GROWTH TYPE: Herbaceous perennial

HARDINESS ZONE: USDA 3 to 8, Sunset all zones

FLOWER COLOR: Metallic blue

HEIGHT: To 5'

BLOOMING PERIOD: July to September

HOW TO GROW: Prefers full sun in a light, well-drained soil, but will tolerate poor soil and drought. Does well with very little attention. An excellent alternative to potentially invasive native and introduced thistles, which are the host plants for the Painted Lady. The Painted Lady will readily use globe thistle for all stages of its life cycle.

BUTTERFLIES ATTRACTED: A wide variety, including Painted Lady, Silver-spotted Skipper, Common Buckeye, Great Spangled Fritillary, Clouded Sulphur.

CULTIVARS AND RELATED SPECIES: *E. ritro*—Small globe thistle, to 2' tall; bright blue flowers.

VIPER'S BUGLOSS • OX-TONGUE

NATIVE HABITAT: Southern Europe
and Asia; open sunny places
GROWTH TYPE: Herbaceous perennial,
usually grown as an annual
HARDINESS ZONE: Grown as an annual
FLOWER COLOR: Blue
HEIGHT: 1 to 3'
BLOOMING PERIOD: June through July
HOW TO GROW: Full sun in well-
drained or dry soils. Spreads rapidly
from creeping rootstocks as well as
from seed. Seeds freely; take care to
control.

BUTTERFLIES ATTRACTED: A wide variety, including the swallowtails, notably
the Eastern Tiger, Spicebush, Black,
Pipevine, Zebra. This plant and others
of its genus serve as larval hosts for
the Common Buckeye.

CULTIVARS AND RELATED SPECIES:
E. vulgare 'Blue Bedder'—1' in height.
E. lycopsis—Blue, mauve and violet
flowers.
E. creticum—Brick-red flowers.

CALIFORNIA FUSCHIA • HUMMINGBIRD FLOWER

NATIVE HABITAT: California coastal
sage scrub, chaparral and oak wood-
land
GROWTH TYPE: Herbaceous perennial
HARDINESS ZONE: USDA 8 to 10,
Sunset 2 to 10, 12 to 24
FLOWER COLOR: Brilliant scarlet
HEIGHT: 1 to 2'
BLOOMING PERIOD: Summer to fall
HOW TO GROW: Full sun, well-drained
soil; little water required. May be
somewhat invasive.

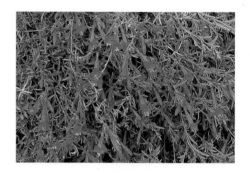

BUTTERFLIES ATTRACTED: A wide variety, including swallowtails.

CULTIVARS AND RELATED SPECIES:
E. c. ssp. latifolium (Z. c. latifolia)—
Mats; 6" tall. Dies back in winter.

COASTAL BUCKWHEAT · CALIFORNIA BUCKWHEAT

NATIVE HABITAT: Coastal sage and chaparral of California

GROWTH TYPE: Perennial spreading or mounding shrub

HARDINESS ZONE: USDA 8 to 9, Sunset 8 and 9, 14 to 24

FLOWER COLOR: White to pink

HEIGHT: 2 to 4'

BLOOMING PERIOD: April to November

HOW TO GROW: Full sun; drought tolerant, needing water only every 3 to 6 weeks when established. (Until then, it should be watered weekly.) Prefers well-drained, loose soil with grainy or sandy composition. May be invasive; useful to cover slopes.

BUTTERFLIES ATTRACTED: Several, including the Common Buckeye, checkerspots, blues, skippers, Painted Lady, swallowtails. Leaves are food for caterpillars of metalmarks and several blues, including the endangered El Segundo Blue (*Euphilotes bernardino allyni*).

CULTIVARS AND RELATED SPECIES: 'Theodore Payne'—Prostrate ground cover.

E. cinereum—Larger clusters of dark pink flowers; more compact form. Favors rocky slopes.

SIBERIAN WALLFLOWER

NATIVE HABITAT: Northern, Central and Eastern Europe; cliffs and rocks

GROWTH TYPE: Biennial

HARDINESS ZONE: USDA 3 to 9, Sunset all zones

FLOWER COLOR: Orange, yellow

HEIGHT: 12 to 18"

BLOOMING PERIOD: Six weeks in spring

HOW TO GROW: Full sun. In hot climates, best grown as a winter flower or with some afternoon shade. Thrives in any soil with average moisture and self-sows. Combine wallflowers with other early-blooming plants, especially tulips. Lovely with pale blue pansies.

BUTTERFLIES ATTRACTED: Several, including whites, blues, swallowtails.

CULTIVARS AND RELATED SPECIES:

E. asperum—4' tall, yellow-flowered western American native that blooms for two months in spring and early summer.

E. linifolium 'E. H. Bowles' and 'Variegatum'—18" tall; purple.

E. capitatum—Cream-colored flowers; West Coast native.

E. cheiri—Yellow, amber or chocolate-maroon single or double flowers in spring. Fragrant. Needs a cool yet mild climate.

JOE-PYE WEED • QUEEN OF THE MEADOW

NATIVE HABITAT: Eastern North America; moist meadows

GROWTH TYPE: Herbaceous perennial

HARDINESS ZONE: USDA 4, Sunset 2 to 9, 14 to 21

FLOWER COLOR: Dusty rose

HEIGHT: To 7'

BLOOMING PERIOD: Late July through August

HOW TO GROW: Full sun in a variety of soil types if given adequate moisture. Does not flourish in warm, southern areas. Plant several and expect a showy display in the third summer.

BUTTERFLIES ATTRACTED: A wide variety, including Painted Lady, Red Admiral, Anise Swallowtail, Milbert's Tortoiseshell, Tiger Swallowtail, Monarch, Silver-spotted Skipper.

CULTIVARS AND RELATED SPECIES: *E. fistulosum*, Hollow Joe-pye weed, and *E. maculatum*, spotted Joe-pye weed—Both resemble *E. purpureum* and are hardy to Zone 3. *E. cannabinum*, Hemp agrimony—4' tall; flowers similar to *E. purpureum*. *E. perfoliatum*, Common boneset—4 to 5' plants with 4" white flowerheads; August blooming.

OCOTILLO

NATIVE HABITAT: Desert Southwest; rocky exposed slopes and dry stream beds, sandy plains
GROWTH TYPE: Deciduous shrub
HARDINESS ZONE: USDA 8, Sunset 10 to 13, 18 to 20
FLOWER COLOR: Red
HEIGHT: To 25'
BLOOMING PERIOD: After rain in spring and summer
HOW TO GROW: Full sun, well-drained soil, little water.
BUTTERFLIES ATTRACTED: Many flying at time of bloom.

GAILLARDIA PULCHELLA

BLANKETFLOWER

NATIVE HABITAT: Central and western North America; dry, sandy areas
GROWTH TYPE: Annual
HARDINESS ZONE: Grown as an annual
FLOWER COLOR: Daisy-like flowers red, tipped with yellow
HEIGHT: To 2'
BLOOMING PERIOD: Summer
HOW TO GROW: Full sun, good drainage. Very salt and drought tolerant. Sow seeds directly into warm soil after frost danger has passed.
BUTTERFLIES ATTRACTED: A wide variety, including Question Mark, Comma, Viceroy, Monarch, Painted Lady, swallowtails, fritillaries, skippers.

WILD GERANIUM

NATIVE HABITAT: Eastern North America; woods and meadows
GROWTH TYPE: Perennial
HARDINESS ZONE: USDA 4 to 8, Sunset 2 to 9, 14 to 21
FLOWER COLOR: Pink
HEIGHT: 1 to 2'
BLOOMING PERIOD: April to early June
HOW TO GROW: Prefers light sun to partial shade in rich, moist, well-drained soil. Requires little maintenance and is not invasive.
BUTTERFLIES ATTRACTED: Small butterflies of open woods and forest edges, such as the Spring Azure and Hobomak Skipper.
CULTIVARS AND RELATED SPECIES:
G. sanguineum, Blood-red geranium—1 to 2' tall; Eurasian native occasionally found escaped from cultivation in eastern U.S.
G. psilostemon—Perennial, 2' tall; dark red blooms. Native to Armenia.

Below: Geranium psilostemon

FIREBUSH

NATIVE HABITAT: Florida and West Indies to South America; margins of hardwood forests

GROWTH TYPE: Evergreen shrub or small tree

HARDINESS ZONE: USDA 8 to 10, Sunset 8 to 24

FLOWER COLOR: Reddish orange

HEIGHT: To 25'

BLOOMING PERIOD: All year

HOW TO GROW: Full sun to partial shade.

BUTTERFLIES ATTRACTED: One of the best native shrubs to attract butterflies in Florida, including large sulphurs, swallowtails, Zebra, Monarch, Gulf Fritillary.

NATIVE HABITAT: North America; wet meadows, thickets

GROWTH TYPE: Perennial

HARDINESS ZONE: USDA 4 to 9, Sunset all zones

FLOWER COLOR: Yellow

HEIGHT: 2-1/2 to 4'

BLOOMING PERIOD: Late July to frost

HOW TO GROW: Requires full sun and moist soil. Prefers average soil, but tolerates poor soil, including wet, heavy clay. Divide when crowded for optimal growth. Does not cause sneezing, but blooms at the same time as ragweed, which does—hence the common name.

BUTTERFLIES ATTRACTED: Several, including Horace's Duskywing.

TAIYO SUNFLOWER

NATIVE HABITAT: From Minnesota and Missouri west to the Pacific; prairies

GROWTH TYPE: Annual

HARDINESS ZONE: Grown as an annual

FLOWER COLOR: Golden yellow, daisy-like flowers

HEIGHT: 5 to 6'

BLOOMING PERIOD: August and September

HOW TO GROW: Full sun in a variety of soils, given moderate moisture. Sow seed in April or May where plants are to grow. Unlike taller sunflowers, will keep heads up without staking.

BUTTERFLIES ATTRACTED: A wide variety, including Monarch, Red Admiral, Lorquin's Admiral, Painted Lady, Western Sulphur.

CULTIVARS AND RELATED SPECIES:
H. annuus, Common sunflower—10' or taller with 12" flowerheads.

H. x *multiflorus,* Many-flowered sunflower—Perennial; 5 to 7' tall with single or sometimes double yellow flowers in fall.

H. angustifolius, Swamp sunflower—Perennial; 5 to 9' tall with abundant 2" yellow flowerheads.

PURPLE HELIOTROPE • CHERRY PIE

NATIVE HABITAT: Peru; mountain and coastal areas, forests

GROWTH TYPE: Tender shrubby perennial

HARDINESS ZONE: USDA 4 to 6, Sunset 8 to 24

FLOWER COLOR: Violet or deep purple

HEIGHT: 1 to 4'

BLOOMING PERIOD: May through September

HOW TO GROW: Full sun, in rich, well-drained soil in pots or in the ground. Sweet vanilla-scented flowers.

BUTTERFLIES ATTRACTED: A wide variety, including Pearl Crescent, Cabbage White, Hayhurst's Scallopwing, Common Sootywing, Horace's Dusky-wing; members of this family serve as larval hosts for the Common Buckeye.

CULTIVARS AND RELATED SPECIES: 'Lemoine'—Tall, with purple flowers. 'Marine'—Short, with violet-purple flowers. 'Regal Dwarf'—Large flowers in blue shades.

HESPERIS MATRONALIS

DAME'S ROCKET • SWEET ROCKET

NATIVE HABITAT: Europe; mountain woods, scrub and by streams
GROWTH TYPE: Herbaceous biennial or perennial
HARDINESS ZONE: USDA 4 to 8, Sunset 2 to 9, 14 to 21
FLOWER COLOR: Purple, sometimes pink, white
HEIGHT: 2 to 3'

BLOOMING PERIOD: May, June
HOW TO GROW: Full sun. Thrives on neglect; reseeds freely. An excellent spring nectar plant for butterflies when little else is available.
BUTTERFLIES ATTRACTED: Several, including swallowtails, whites, sulphurs, Painted Lady, Monarch.

CHINESE HIBISCUS

NATIVE HABITAT: Tropical areas; disturbed sites, riversides
GROWTH TYPE: Evergreen shrub
HARDINESS ZONE: USDA 9 to 10, Sunset 9, 12, 13, 15, 16, 19 to 24
FLOWER COLOR: White, yellow, pinks, corals, red
HEIGHT: 15'

BLOOMING PERIOD: Summer
HOW TO GROW: Needs heat to thrive. Best grown in pots so that it can be protected in cold weather. Needs rich soil, good drainage, monthly fertilizing from April to September. Water once or twice a week.
BUTTERFLIES ATTRACTED: A wide variety, including Cloudless Sulphur, Western Tiger Swallowtail, blues, hairstreaks, Gulf Fritillary.
CULTIVARS AND RELATED SPECIES: Many; the red-flowered hibiscus may be especially attractive to butterflies.

HYLOTELEPHIUM (SEDUM) SPECTABILE 'METEOR'

SEDUM

NATIVE HABITAT: China, Japan; dry, grassy places in scrub and by rocky streams
GROWTH TYPE: Herbaceous perennial
HARDINESS ZONE: USDA 3 to 9, Sunset all zones
FLOWER COLOR: Pink

HEIGHT: 1 to 2'
BLOOMING PERIOD: August through September
HOW TO GROW: Full sun, light shade in well-drained soil, average water. Will thrive in poor soil.
BUTTERFLIES ATTRACTED: One of the best fall nectar sources; attracts a wide variety of butterflies, including swallowtails, sulphurs, coppers, hairstreaks, blues, nymphalids, Monarch, skippers.
CULTIVARS AND RELATED SPECIES: 'Carmen'—Soft rose. 'Autumn Joy' is a popular cultivar, but may not be attractive to butterflies.

BALSAM

NATIVE HABITAT: India, China and Malay Peninsula; wet, often open areas
GROWTH TYPE: Summer annual
HARDINESS ZONE: Grown as an annual
FLOWER COLOR: Pink, rose, lilac, red
HEIGHT: 8 to 30"
BLOOMING PERIOD: Summer
HOW TO GROW: Full sun; water frequently. Sow seed indoors in early spring.
BUTTERFLIES ATTRACTED: Many, including swallowtails, Cabbage White, Gulf Fritillary; a larval host plant for Painted Lady.

PEREGRINA

NATIVE HABITAT: Cuba and tropical South America; dry or sandy areas, vacant lots and disturbed sites
GROWTH TYPE: Shrub or small tree
HARDINESS ZONE: USDA 9 to 10, Sunset 16 to 17, 21 to 24
FLOWER COLOR: Scarlet or rose
HEIGHT: 3 to 10'
BLOOMING PERIOD: All year
HOW TO GROW: Full sun.
BUTTERFLIES ATTRACTED: Swallowtails, sulphurs, Monarch, Queen, skippers.
CULTIVARS AND RELATED SPECIES:
J. multifida, Coral plant—Shrub to 12'; red flowers; yellow, poisonous fruit.

J. podagrica, Gout plant—Single-stemmed shrub to 5' tall; male flowers scarlet.

LANTANA · SHRUB VERBENA

NATIVE HABITAT: Tropical and subtropical North and South America; forest margins, disturbed sites
GROWTH TYPE: Evergreen or deciduous shrub
HARDINESS ZONE: USDA 9 to 10, Sunset 12 to 13, 15 to 22
FLOWER COLOR: Yellow, orange, red
HEIGHT: 2 to 6'
BLOOMING PERIOD: All year in frost-free areas; summer elsewhere
HOW TO GROW: Full sun, any soil. Water infrequently but thoroughly. Can be invasive in warm climates.
BUTTERFLIES ATTRACTED: Attracts a wide variety.
CULTIVARS AND RELATED SPECIES: *L. montevidensis*, Trailing lantana—A good ground cover with rosy-lilac flowers. Many cultivars of both species are available.

DAISY · OX-EYE DAISY

Tanacetum coccineum, Pyrethrum or painted daisy—1 to 2' tall.
T. parthenium, Feverfew or matricaria—1 to 2-1/2' tall; annual.

NATIVE HABITAT: Eurasia; fields
GROWTH TYPE: Short-lived perennial
HARDINESS ZONE: USDA 3 to 9, Sunset 4 to 24
FLOWER COLOR: Yellow center surrounded by white rays
HEIGHT: 1 to 2'
BLOOMING PERIOD: June to August
HOW TO GROW: Full sun, ordinary soil.
BUTTERFLIES ATTRACTED: Several, including American Copper, Early Hairstreak, Atlantis Fritillary, European Skipper.
CULTIVARS AND RELATED SPECIES: *L.* x *superbum*, Shasta daisy—1 to 2' tall.

GAYFEATHER • BLAZING STAR

NATIVE HABITAT: Eastern and Central United States; moist meadows, fertile grasslands

GROWTH TYPE: Herbaceous perennial

HARDINESS ZONE: USDA 4 to 9, Sunset 1 to 3, 7 to 10, 14 to 24

FLOWER COLOR: Rose-purple

HEIGHT: 2 to 4'

BLOOMING PERIOD: Late summer for three weeks

HOW TO GROW: Full sun and deep, well-drained but moist soil. Plant gayfeather with its crown at soil level or it will rot. Combine with big bluestem grass, rudbeckia, purple coneflower for an evocative North American grassland combination. A good cut flower.

BUTTERFLIES ATTRACTED: Painted Lady, fritillaries, checkerspots, coppers, crescents, sulphurs, skippers.

CULTIVARS AND RELATED SPECIES:
'Floristan white'—3' tall.
'Kobold'—18" tall.
L. punctata—12" tall; drought tolerant.
L. pycnostachya, Prairie gayfeather—5' tall.

STATICE

NATIVE HABITAT: Mediterranean; fields and scrub

GROWTH TYPE: Half-hardy biennial grown as an annual

HARDINESS ZONE: Grown as an annual

FLOWER COLOR: White, blue, lavender, yellow, pink, red

HEIGHT: 1 to 2-1/2'

BLOOMING PERIOD: Mid to late summer

HOW TO GROW: Full sun in well-drained, light, sandy, infertile soil. Tolerates heat, drought, salt spray. Sow outdoors after frost or indoors in spring. Tolerates transplanting better when small. Excellent cut and dried flower.

BUTTERFLIES ATTRACTED: Several, including Clouded Sulphur, Painted Lady.

CULTIVARS AND RELATED SPECIES: *L. latifolium,* Hardy statice—1-1/2 to 2' tall; semi-evergreen; leathery leaves.

DEERWEED

NATIVE HABITAT: Dry coastal sage scrub and chaparral in California

GROWTH TYPE: Perennial shrub

HARDINESS ZONE: USDA 9 to 10, Sunset 14 to 24

FLOWER COLOR: Bright yellow, maturing to orange and red

HEIGHT: 3'

BLOOMING PERIOD: All year

HOW TO GROW: Full sun, rocky or sandy soils, little water. Small, sparse leaflets and delicate sweet pea-shaped flowers make a nice contrast with the larger foliage of garden plants. Its name is derived from the belief that deer and cattle relish it.

BUTTERFLIES ATTRACTED: One of the best butterfly plants for the West, attracting several species of whites, blues, hairstreaks, Painted Lady, skippers. A larval host of several species.

RUSSELL LUPINES

Native habitat: Hybrid

Growth type: Perennial

Hardiness Zone: USDA 3 to 7, Sunset 1 to 7, 14 to 17

Flower color: Blue, pink, red, white; often bicolor

Height: 2 to 4'

Blooming period: Mid spring to midsummer

How to grow: Full sun or partial shade with a neutral, well-drained soil, not too rich. Does best in cool summer areas and humid climates. Resents transplanting; sow seed directly out-doors in early spring. May be short-lived but may self-seed.

Butterflies attracted: Several, including Canadian Tiger Swallowtail and Monarch; lupines are larval hosts for various blues.

Cultivars and related species: *L. perennis*, Wild lupine—1 to 2' perennial; the only eastern North American native. Only larval host for the rare Karner Blue.

L. subcarnosus and *L. texensis*—1 to 2' annuals.

NATIVE HABITAT: South Dakota to Alberta, south to north-central Mexico; sandy soils, stream beds

GROWTH TYPE: Herbaceous annual

HARDINESS ZONE: Annual

FLOWER COLOR: Purple, pinkish-white

HEIGHT: To 16"

BLOOMING PERIOD: May to frost

HOW TO GROW: Full sun in any good garden soil. Use only light fertilizer; keep on dry side and deadhead to maximize flowering. Plant in masses.

BUTTERFLIES ATTRACTED: Many, especially skippers and hairstreaks.

CULTIVARS AND RELATED SPECIES: *M. bigelovii*, Purple aster—Western U.S. native; grows to 3' tall. Purple to violet flowerheads from March to November.

MONKEY FLOWER

NATIVE HABITAT: Oregon, California, Nevada, Arizona; riparian or woodland areas below 2,000 feet

GROWTH TYPE: Herbaceous perennial

HARDINESS ZONE: USDA 7 to 10, Sunset 4 to 24

FLOWER COLOR: Scarlet red

HEIGHT: 1 to 3'

BLOOMING PERIOD: April to October

HOW TO GROW: Partial shade, well-drained soil, regular watering. Drought tolerant, but looks better in gardens if given some water. May be pruned after flowering to prolong bloom.

BUTTERFLIES ATTRACTED: Several, including checkerspots, ringlets, Painted Lady, Cabbage White, Checkered White.

CULTIVARS AND RELATED SPECIES:
M. aurantiacus, Sticky monkey flower—3 to 6' tall, bushy. Pale apricot-colored flowers. Native to southern coastal California. Larval food plant for Common Buckeye and Chalcedon Checkerspot.

M. a. rutilus, Sticky monkey flower—Naturally occurring variety with red flowers.

M. guttatus—Yellow flowers January to July.

BEE BALM · SWEET BERGAMOT · OSWEGO TEA

NATIVE HABITAT: Eastern North America; moist, fertile woodlands
GROWTH TYPE: Herbaceous perennial
HARDINESS ZONE: USDA 4 to 9, Sunset all zones
FLOWER COLOR: Red
HEIGHT: 4'
BLOOMING PERIOD: July to August
HOW TO GROW: Full sun in northern gardens, afternoon shade in southern gardens. Average or rich soil. Deep mulching is advised. Divide clumps every third year.
BUTTERFLIES ATTRACTED: Various species, including Lorquin's Admiral, Painted Lady, Cabbage White, Milbert's Tortoiseshell, Clodius Parnassian.
CULTIVARS AND RELATED SPECIES:
'Croftway Pink'—Soft pink flowers.
'Beauty of Cobham'—Light pink flowers.
M. fistulosa, Wild bergamot—Lavender flowers. Taller and more drought tolerant than *M. didyma*. Blooms throughout August.
M. citriodora, Lemon mint—Rich pink flowers; 2 to 3' in height; annual or biennial. Full sun and dry soil. Blooms July to August.

GIANT CATMINT

NATIVE HABITAT: Siberia; dry habitats
GROWTH TYPE: Herbaceous perennial
HARDINESS ZONE: USDA 3 to 8, Sunset 4 to 24
FLOWER COLOR: Spode blue
HEIGHT: 3 to 4'
BLOOMING PERIOD: All summer
HOW TO GROW: Sun with afternoon shade in hot summer climates. Well-drained soil with average moisture is best. One of the best summer-blooming perennials, with pungently fragrant foliage of no interest to cats. Self sows; can become invasive in fertile, loose soil. Combine with old-garden and shrub roses.
BUTTERFLIES ATTRACTED: Swallowtails, fritillaries, Painted Lady, Viceroy, Red Admiral, Checkered White.
CULTIVARS AND RELATED SPECIES: 'Blue Beauty' ('Souvenir d'André Chaudron')—Compact, 18" tall.

PASSION FLOWER VINE

NATIVE HABITAT: Hybrid

GROWTH TYPE: Vine, evergreen in tropics and subtropics

HARDINESS ZONE: USDA 9 to 10, Sunset 5 to 9, 12 to 24

FLOWER COLOR: Bloom is a pattern of white, purple and blue

HEIGHT: Vine

BLOOMING PERIOD: All summer

HOW TO GROW: Full sun, average watering in a mulched soil. Protect against wind and frost. Best grown in a pot and trained on a trellis; put water in the pot's tray to discourage ants and therefore aphids. Prune dead branches, but do not cut off shoots leading to new growth since these are used by egg-laying butterflies.

BUTTERFLIES ATTRACTED: Gulf Fritillary, Cabbage White, Painted Lady; larval host for the Gulf Fritillary and other heliconians.

CULTIVARS AND RELATED SPECIES: Although it has attractive flowers, *P.* x *alato-caerulea* is the least attractive to egg-laying butterflies. *P. manicata*, with scarlet flowers, or *P. jamesonii* 'Coral sea' are hosts to caterpillars of the Gulf Fritillary. *P.* 'Incense' may be one of the best passion flower vines for butterfly gardening.

PENTAS • STARFLOWER

NATIVE HABITAT: Tropical Africa; open areas, forest margins

GROWTH TYPE: Perennial shrub grown as an annual

HARDINESS ZONE: Grown as an annual

FLOWER COLOR: Magenta, pink, red, lilac, white

HEIGHT: To 4'

BLOOMING PERIOD: All year

HOW TO GROW: Full sun to partial shade, ample water and fertilizer. Use as an annual in cold temperate regions, evergreen shrub in southern states. Best used in mass plantings to add vibrant color to the landscape.

BUTTERFLIES ATTRACTED: One of the best butterfly-attracting plants; sulphurs, swallowtails, Monarch, fritillaries, skippers.

GARDEN PHLOX • SUMMER PHLOX

NATIVE HABITAT: Eastern and Central United States; woodland edges
GROWTH TYPE: Herbaceous perennial
HARDINESS ZONE: USDA 4 to 8, Sunset 1 to 14, 18 to 21
FLOWER COLOR: Pink, white, rose, lilac, salmon, scarlet, purple
HEIGHT: 3 to 5'
BLOOMING PERIOD: Mid to late summer for 4 to 6 weeks
HOW TO GROW: Morning sun and afternoon shade except in the coolest climates, where full sun all day is best. Thrives in rich, moist but well-drained soil. Good air circulation and watering at ground level help minimize powdery mildew. Garden phlox has a sweet, gentle fragrance and makes a good cut flower. Its showy flowers are the mainstay of many perennial plantings during the dog days of summer.
BUTTERFLIES ATTRACTED: Swallowtails, sulphurs, Painted Lady, Viceroy, Red Admiral.
CULTIVARS AND RELATED SPECIES:
'Bright Eyes'—Pink blooms with red eyes.
'Dodo Hanbury Forbes'—Pink flowers.
P. maculata—Blooms a month earlier and is more mildew resistant. Cultivars include 'Alpha' and 'Rosalinde' (rose-pink flowers).
P. divaricata, Wild blue phlox—Spring-blooming ground cover from the Appalachians; white or blue flowers are quite atttractive to early butterflies.

81

ORCHID PRIMROSE

NATIVE HABITAT: Northwestern China; marshy fields at altitudes up to 9,000 feet
GROWTH TYPE: Herbaceous perennial
HARDINESS ZONE: USDA 5 to 9, Sunset 1 to 6, 17
FLOWER COLOR: Lilac blue flowers, showy scarlet calyces
HEIGHT: 2'
BLOOMING PERIOD: Early summer for five weeks
HOW TO GROW: Only morning sun in moist, humus-rich soil.
BUTTERFLIES ATTRACTED: Various, including Clodius Parnassian, Pale Swallowtail, West Coast Lady, Western

Tiger Swallowtail, Mourning Cloak.
CULTIVARS AND RELATED SPECIES:
P. japonica, Japanese primrose—15 to 30" tall.
P.j. 'Postford White'—Pristine white blossoms.

HEAL-ALL • SELFHEAL

NATIVE HABITAT: Eurasia; forests, forest edges, dry meadows, irrigation ditches, lakeshores
GROWTH TYPE: Herbaceous perennial
HARDINESS ZONE: USDA 4 to 9, Sunset 1 to 21
FLOWER COLOR: Lavender, purple

HEIGHT: Under 1'
BLOOMING PERIOD: June to September
HOW TO GROW: Full sun to partial shade in ordinary garden soil with average moisture. Self-sows easily.
BUTTERFLIES ATTRACTED: Several, including Spicebush Swallowtail, Clouded Sulphur, Orange Sulphur, Cabbage White, Silver-spotted Skipper.
CULTIVARS AND RELATED SPECIES:
P. grandiflora 'Alba'—White flowers. There are also pink and pale lavender cultivars.

MOUNTAIN MINT

NATIVE HABITAT: Throughout North America; dry woods, thickets, fields and uplands

GROWTH TYPE: Herbaceous perennial

HARDINESS ZONE: USDA 4 to 8, Sunset 2 to 9, 14 to 21

FLOWER COLOR: White with pink flecks

HEIGHT: 3'

BLOOMING PERIOD: Summer to frost

HOW TO GROW: Full sun in any soil.

BUTTERFLIES ATTRACTED: Most butterflies flying during the blooming period.

CULTIVARS AND RELATED SPECIES: *Pycnanthemum pilosum*—Like *P. muticum,* but with narrower leaves.

BLACK-EYED SUSAN

NATIVE HABITAT: Throughout North America; dry fields, open woods, roadsides and waste places

GROWTH TYPE: Biennial or short-lived perennial

HARDINESS ZONE: USDA 3 to 10, Sunset all zones

FLOWER COLOR: Dark brown center with yellow-gold rays

HEIGHT: 2 to 3'

BLOOMING PERIOD: June to August

HOW TO GROW: Full sun or light shade in average, well-drained soil. Tolerates poor soil, drought and neglect. Easily grown from seed; may bloom first year from seed and readily self-seeds. Can be invasive, so pick off flower heads after blooming to prevent self-seeding.

BUTTERFLIES ATTRACTED: Many, including blues, Great Spangled Fritillary, Silver-bordered Fritillary, Meadow Fritillary, Pearl Crescent, Viceroy, Monarch; the Silvery Checkerspot uses this plant as a caterpillar food plant.

CULTIVARS AND RELATED SPECIES: *R. hirta* 'Gloriosa', Gloriosa daisy—2 to 4' tall; spectacular two-toned rays. Does not grow true from seed.

R. laciniata, Green-headed coneflower—3 to 8' tall; moist soil; sun or shade.

R. fulgida, Orange coneflower—2 to 4' tall; 'Goldsturm' is popular.

R. triloba, Thin-leaved coneflower—3 to 4' tall; tolerates drought and partial shade.

SCARLET SAGE · RED SALVIA

NATIVE HABITAT: Southeastern United States, West Indies, tropical America; dry or stony sites

GROWTH TYPE: Herbaceous perennial or subshrub

HARDINESS ZONE: USDA 8 to 10, Sunset 7 to 24

FLOWER COLOR: Red, rarely white

HEIGHT: 2 to 3'

BLOOMING PERIOD: All year in warm climates; summer in cold, temperate regions

HOW TO GROW: Full sun; easy to grow.

BUTTERFLIES ATTRACTED: Several, including Monarch, Queen, sulphurs, swallowtails, fritillaries.

CULTIVARS AND RELATED SPECIES:
S. greggii —3- to 4'-tall perennial shrub; native to Texas and Mexico. Red with pink and salmon forms available. Blooms late spring to summer; fall in desert.

S. leucophylla, Purple sage—3- to 5'-tall perennial shrub; native to southern California. Pink to lavender blooms May to July.

S. spathacea, Hummingbird or pitcher sage—Perennial; native to west coast oak woodlands. Blooms March to May.

BLUE PINCUSHION FLOWER

Native habitat: Europe, Africa, Asia, Caucasus; dry meadows, herbaceous slopes, scrub, forest edges
Growth type: Herbaceous perennial
Hardiness zone: USDA 4 to 8, Sunset 4 to 24
Flower color: Powder blue
Height: 12"
Blooming period: Summer into fall
How to grow: Full sun in well-drained, lean soil on the dry side. Excellent cut flower and easy to combine in any color scheme. 'Butterfly Blue' and 'Pink Mist' are great performers throughout the United States.
Butterflies attracted: Swallowtails, whites, sulphurs, Painted Lady, Red Admiral.
Cultivars and related species: 'Pink Mist'—Pink, long-lasting flowers.
S. caucasica—Coarser with larger but less numerous flowers; less well suited to hot climates. Cultivars include 'Bressingham White', 'Clive Greaves' (blue flowers with white centers), 'Fama' (deeper blue blooms).

SEASIDE GOLDENROD

NATIVE HABITAT: Coastal Newfoundland to New Jersey

GROWTH TYPE: Herbaceous perennial

HARDINESS ZONE: USDA 4 to 7, Sunset all zones

FLOWER COLOR: Yellow

HEIGHT: 5 to 7'

BLOOMING PERIOD: Late August to September

HOW TO GROW: Full sun, lean soil, average water. Good for meadow plantings. Staking may be necessary.

BUTTERFLIES ATTRACTED: A wide variety, especially Monarch.

CULTIVARS AND RELATED SPECIES: Many, including:

S. graminifolia, Lance-leaved goldenrod—The common flat-topped goldenrod; grasslike leaves; to 4' tall.

S. rigida, Hard-leaved goldenrod—Stiff growth habit; relatively large flowers; to 5' tall.

BLUE PORTERWEED

NATIVE HABITAT: Florida, West Indies and tropical America; pinelands and disturbed sites
GROWTH TYPE: Shrub or annual or perennial herb
HARDINESS ZONE: USDA 9 to 10, Sunset 14 to 24
FLOWER COLOR: Blue
HEIGHT: To 3'

BLOOMING PERIOD: Spring to autumn
HOW TO GROW: Full sun to partial shade.
BUTTERFLIES ATTRACTED: Sulphurs, swallowtails, fritillaries, skippers, Monarch.
CULTIVARS AND RELATED SPECIES: Other species with dark blue, pink and violet flowers are available in southern Florida.

NATIVE HABITAT: Southeast Europe; mixed scrub at elevations of about 3,500 feet

GROWTH TYPE: Deciduous shrub

HARDINESS ZONE: USDA 3 to 7, Sunset 1 to 11

FLOWER COLOR: Purple, white, pink, lavender

HEIGHT: To 10'

BLOOMING PERIOD: May

HOW TO GROW: Full sun in well-drained soil. Most require winter chill; some hybrids are adapted to warmer climates.

BUTTERFLIES ATTRACTED: Spring nectar source when little else is available; attracts swallowtails, nymphalids, Monarch.

CULTIVARS AND RELATED SPECIES: There are hundreds of different cultivars of the common lilac. Take the time to select a cultivar that is compact, has fragrant flowers and is disease resistant.

FRENCH MARIGOLD

NATIVE HABITAT: Mexico; roadsides and open woodland

GROWTH TYPE: Annual

HARDINESS ZONE: Grown as an annual

FLOWER COLOR: Yellow, orange, bronze, rust red

HEIGHT: 1/2 to 1-1/2'

BLOOMING PERIOD: Throughout summer until frost

HOW TO GROW: Sun in well-drained, moist soil. Remove spent flowerheads to extend bloom. Look for single-flowered varieties for best nectar availability.

BUTTERFLIES ATTRACTED: Several, including Clouded Sulphur, American Lady, West Coast Lady, Milbert's Tortoiseshell, Satchem, Nysa Roadside-Skipper.

MEXICAN SUNFLOWER

NATIVE HABITAT: Mexico and Central America; roadsides and thickets

GROWTH TYPE: Perennial grown as a summer annual

HARDINESS ZONE: Grown as an annual

FLOWER COLOR: Yellow centers, orange rays

HEIGHT: 6'

BLOOMING PERIOD: July to frost

HOW TO GROW: Sun in lean soil. Tolerates drought; good in desert gardens. Sow seed directly outdoors in spring. Staking may be necessary. Deadhead to extend flowering period.

BUTTERFLIES ATTRACTED: A great butterfly-attracting plant; wide variety, including swallowtails.

CULTIVARS AND RELATED SPECIES: 'Torch'—4' tall; orange flowered. 'Sundance'—3' tall; orange flowers.

VERBENA

Native habitat: South America; wet fields and disturbed areas

Growth type: Herbaceous perennial

Hardiness zone: USDA 7 to 10, Sunset 4 to 24

Flower color: Lavender

Height: 3 to 4'

Blooming period: Late June to frost

How to grow: Sun; grown as an annual in the North.

Butterflies attracted: A wide variety, including swallowtails and sulphurs.

Above, verbena cultivar

Cultivars and related species:

V. bipinnatifida—8- to 15"-tall perennial; native to western Great Plains to Mexico. Lavender flowers all summer; self-seeds.

V. rigida—10- to 20"-tall perennial. Lilac to purple-blue blooms, summer to fall.

V. tenuisecta, Purple moss verbena—Annual; South American native. Blue-purple violet flowers.

NATIVE HABITAT: Massachusetts to Mississippi, Ohio; low thickets, streambanks

GROWTH TYPE: Herbaceous perennial

HARDINESS ZONE: USDA 4 to 8, Sunset 14 to 21

FLOWER COLOR: Purple

HEIGHT: To 6'

BLOOMING PERIOD: Late summer and autumn

HOW TO GROW: Full sun, most soils as long as they are moist. Interplant with other moisture-loving natives, such as cardinal flower, boneset and mistflower for an attractive butterfly habitat.

BUTTERFLIES ATTRACTED: Many, including Eastern Tiger Swallowtail, Monarch, Great Spangled Fritillary, American Lady, Silver-spotted Skipper, Spicebush Swallowtail.

CULTIVARS AND RELATED SPECIES: 'Purple Haze'—Open clusters of deep violet flowers; grows to 8'.

V. gigantea—Grows to 10'.

CHASTE TREE • INDIAN SPICE • SAGE-TREE

NATIVE HABITAT: Western Europe and Asia; riverbanks, streambanks, irrigation ditches

GROWTH TYPE: Large shrub to small tree

HARDINESS ZONE: USDA 7 to 10, Sunset 4 to 24

FLOWER COLOR: White, blue, purple, pink

HEIGHT: 10 to 20'

BLOOMING PERIOD: May to September

HOW TO GROW: Full sun in poor to fair, well-drained soil. Restrict watering. Fertilize sparingly in spring with high-phosphorus fertilizer to increase blooming. Prune vigorously to maintain as a shrub. Protect from severe cold temperatures.

BUTTERFLIES ATTRACTED: Almost all butterflies flying when it flowers, including hairstreaks, blues and swallowtails.

CULTIVARS AND RELATED SPECIES:
'Caerulea'—Blue flowers.
'Alba'—White fowers.
V. a.-c. rosea—Pink flowers.

NATIVE HABITAT: Mexico; woodland openings, grassy and weedy areas, old fields, roadsides and ditches, in open oak forest or tropical deciduous forest

GROWTH TYPE: Herbaceous annual

HARDINESS ZONE: Grown as an annual

FLOWER COLOR: Pink, salmon, rose, red, yellow, orange, lavender, purple, green

HEIGHT: 1 to 3'

BLOOMING PERIOD: June to October

HOW TO GROW: Full sun in well-drained garden soil. Feed and water frequently; avoid overhead water to discourage powdery mildew. Sow directly outdoors. Deadhead to maintain blooming. Plant in big, thick patches.

BUTTERFLIES ATTRACTED: Almost all groups, including swallowtails, sulphurs, coppers, hairstreaks, blues, nymphalids, Monarch, skippers.

CULTIVARS AND RELATED SPECIES: Many forms are available; look for single flowers to increase nectar availability. Taller varieties may be more attractive to butterflies.

Following are the butterflies most likely to be found in gardens in different regions of the country. For scientific names and further information on identifying butterflies in your garden, see the Encyclopedia of Butterflies beginning on page 15. For information on species that are not featured in this book, consult the field guides listed in the bibliography on page 103.

NORTHEAST

Great Spangled Fritillary
American Lady
Spring Azure
Eastern Tailed Blue
Eastern Tiger Swallowtail
White Admiral
Viceroy

Cabbage White
Clouded Sulphur
Pearl Crescent
Monarch
Gray Comma
Comma
Question Mark
Red Admiral
Mourning Cloak
Viceroy
Black Swallowtail
Milbert's Tortoiseshell

SOUTHEAST

Eastern Tiger Swallowtail
Gulf Fritillary
Question Mark
Red-spotted Purple

Above: Gulf Fritillary
Right: Question Mark

Viceroy
Sleepy Orange
Great Spangled Fritillary
Buckeye
Monarch
Silver-spotted Skipper
Orange Sulphur
Gray Hairstreak
American Lady
Pearl Crescent
Eastern Tailed Blue
Spring Azure
Cabbage White

Buckeye

SUBTROPICAL FLORIDA

Eastern Tiger Swallowtail
Gulf Fritillary
Zebra
Giant Swallowtail
Cloudless Sulphur
Buckeye
Long-tailed Skipper
Red Admiral
American Lady
Pearl Crescent
Spicebush Swallowtail

MIDWEST

Cabbage White
Checkered White
Orange Sulphur
Clouded Sulphur
Eastern Tiger Swallowtail
Eastern Black Swallowtail

Pearl Crescent
Eastern Tailed Blue
Spring Azure
Monarch
American Lady
Viceroy
Red-spotted Purple
Great Spangled Fritillary
Question Mark
Comma

ROCKY MOUNTAINS/GREAT BASIN

Painted Lady
Two-tailed Swallowtail
Aphrodite Fritillary
Red Admiral
Silver-spotted Skipper
Cabbage White
Checkered White
Weidemeyer's Admiral
Pearl Crescent
Eastern Black Swallowtail
Milbert's Tortoiseshell
Field Crescent

COMMON BUTTERFLIES BY REGION

DESERT SOUTHWEST

Two-tailed Swallowtail
Eastern Black Swallowtail
Giant Swallowtail
Orange Sulphur
Sleepy Orange
Cabbage White
Checkered White
Gray Hairstreak
Buckeye
Gulf Fritillary
Monarch
Painted Lady
Red Admiral

SOUTHERN COASTAL CALIFORNIA

Cabbage White
Checkered White
Orange Sulphur
Gray Hairstreak
Buckeye
Gulf Fritillary
Monarch
Painted Lady
West Coast Lady
Mylitta Crescent
Lorquin's Admiral

PACIFIC NORTHWEST

Orange Sulphur
Cabbage White
Checkered White
Spring Azure
Purplish Copper
Mourning Cloak
West Coast Lady
Red Admiral
Lorquin's Admiral
Painted Lady

Above: Two-tailed
Swallowtail
Right: Viceroy

RECOMMENDED BUTTERFLY PLANTS BY REGION

Following are ten outstanding butterfly-attracting plants to try for each major region of the country. See the Encyclopedia of Plants, page 36, for descriptive information about these and other plants and how to grow them.

NORTHEAST

Asclepias spp—Milkweeds
Aster spp—Asters
Buddleia davidii—Butterfly bush
Clethra alnifolia—
   Sweet pepperbush
Echinacea purpurea—
   Purple coneflower
Eupatorium spp—Joe-pye weeds
Pycnanthemum muticum—
   Mountain mint
Tithonia rotundifolia—
   Mexican sunflower
Verbena spp—Verbenas
Zinnia spp—Zinnias

MID-ATLANTIC

Asclepias spp—Milkweeds
Aster novae-angliae—
   New England aster
Buddleia davidii—Butterfly bush
Echinacea purpurea—
   Purple coneflower
Eupatorium spp—Joe-pye weeds
Solidago spp—Goldenrods
Tithonia rotundifolia—
   Mexican sunflower
Verbena bonariensis—Verbena
Vernonia noveboracensis—
   Ironweed
Zinnia spp—Zinnias

Left: Ocotillo
Below: Blanketflower

99

RECOMMENDED BUTTERFLY PLANTS BY REGION

SOUTHEAST

Abelia x *grandiflora*—Glossy abelia
Asclepias spp—Butterfly weeds
Buddleia davidii—Butterfly bush
Lantana spp—Lantanas
Liatris spp—Gayfeathers
Pentas lanceolata—Starflower
Phlox paniculata—Summer phlox
Tithonia rotundifolia—
    Mexican sunflower
Verbena spp—Verbenas
Vitex agnus-castus—Chaste tree

SUBTROPICAL FLORIDA

Duranta erecta—Golden dewdrop
Gaillardia spp—Blanket flowers
Hamelia patens—Firebush
Jatropha integerrima—Peregrina
Lantana spp—Lantanas
Liatris spp—Gayfeathers
Pentas lanceolata—Starflower
Salvia coccinea—Scarlet sage
Stachytarpheta jamaicensis—
    Blue porterweed
Tithonia rotundifolia—
    Mexican sunflower

MIDWEST

Apocynum androsaemifolium—
    Dogbane
Asclepias spp—Butterfly weeds
Aster spp—Asters
Ceanothus americanus—
    New Jersey tea
Echinacea spp—Purple coneflowers
Liatris spp—Gayfeathers
Monarda spp—Bee balms
Nepeta cataria—Catnip

Above: Chaste tree
Right: Starflower

Solidago spp—Goldenrods
Tagetes spp—Marigolds

ROCKY MOUNTAINS/GREAT PLAINS

Amorpha canescens—Lead plant
Asclepias tuberosa—Butterfly weed
Buddleia spp—Butterfly bushes
Centranthus ruber—Red valerian
Ceratostigma plumbaginoides—
  Leadwort
Erysimum spp—Wallflowers
Liatris spp—Gayfeathers
Phlox paniculata—Garden phlox

Red-banded Hairstreak on milkweed

Scabiosa spp—Pincushion flowers
Verbena spp—Verbenas

SOUTHWEST

Agastache cana—Wild hyssop
Asclepias spp—Milkweeds
Chilopsis linearis—Desert willow
Chrysothamnus nauseosus—
  Rabbitbrush
Fouquieria splendens—Ocotillo

Lantana spp—Lantanas
Machaeranthera bigelovii—
  Purple aster
Machaeranthera tanacetifolia—
  Tansy aster
Salvia greggii—Cherry sage
Verbena spp—Verbenas

SOUTHERN COASTAL CALIFORNIA

Asclepias spp—Milkweeds
Eriogonum fasciculatum—
  Coastal Buckwheat
Impatiens spp—Impatiens
Lantana spp—Lantanas
Lotus scoparius—Deerweed
Mimulus spp—Monkey flowers
Rosmarinus spp—Rosemarys
Solidago spp—Goldenrods
Tagetes spp—Marigolds
Zinnia spp—Zinnias

PACIFIC NORTHWEST

Achillea spp—Yarrows
Agastache foeniculum—Anise hyssop
Buddleia spp—Butterfly bushes
Centranthus ruber—Red valerian
Dianthus spp—Pinks
Eupatorium purpureum—
  Joe-pye weed
Helianthus 'Taiyo'—Sunflower
Monarda spp—Bee balms
Phlox paniculata—Phlox
Hylotelephium spectabile—
  Stonecrop

WHERE TO SEE BUTTERFLY GARDENS

The Butterfly Place
Papillon Park
120 Tyngsboro Road
Westford, MA 01886
508-392-0955

Cape May Bird Observatory
P. O. Box 3
Cape May Point, NJ 08212
609-884-2736

The Day Butterfly Center
Callaway Gardens
Pine Mountain, GA 31822-2000
706-663-2281

Butterfly World
Tradewinds Park
3600 West Sample Road
Coconut Creek, FL 33073
305-977-4400

The Cockerell Butterfly Center
Houston Museum of Natural Science
One Herman Circle Drive
Houston, TX 77030
713-639-4678

San Diego Wild Animal Park
15500 San Pasqual Valley Road
Escondido, CA 92027-9614
619-480-9573

Okanagon Butterfly World
1190 Stevens Road
Kelowna, British Columbia
Canada V1Z 1G1
604-769-4408

For a complete list of gardens in the U.S. and Canada, consult *Where Are the Butterfly Gardens?* ($5.75 from The Lepidopterists' Society, 1013 Great Springs Road, Rosemont, PA 19010).

SOCIETIES

North American Butterfly Association
4 Delaware Rd.
Morristown, NJ 07960

The Lepidopterists' Society
1900 John Street
Manhattan Beach, CA 90266-2608

The Xerces Society
10 Southwest Ash St.
Portland, OR 97024

Young Entomologists' Society, Inc.
1915 Peggy Place
Lansing, MI 48910-2553

BIBLIOGRAPHY

Ajilvsgi, Geyata. *Butterfly Gardening for the South.* Taylor Publishing Company, Dallas. 1990.

Glassberg, J. *Butterflies through Binoculars: A Field Guide to Butterflies in the Boston-New York-Washington Region.* Oxford University Press, New York. 1993.

Opler, P. A. and G. O. Krizek. *Butterflies East of the Great Plains.* Johns Hopkins Press, Baltimore. 1984.

Pyle, R. M. *The Audubon Society Field Guide to North American Butterflies.* Knopf, New York. 1981.

Pyle, R. M. *The Audubon Society Handbook for Butterfly Watchers.* Charles Scribner's Sons, New York. 1984.

Scott, J. A. *The Butterflies of North America.* Stanford University Press, Stanford. 1986.

Stokes, Donald, Lillian Stokes and Ernest Williams. *The Butterfly Book: An Easy Guide to Butterfly Gardening, Identification and Behavior.* Little, Brown and Company, Boston. 1991.

Tekulsky, M. *The Butterfly Garden.* The Harvard Common Press, Boston. 1985.

Xerces Society/Smithsonian Institution. *Butterfly Gardening: Creating Summer Magic in Your Garden.* Sierra Club Books, San Francisco. 1990.

PHOTO CREDITS

Cover and pages 8 (all), 9 (all), 44, 47 top, 53, 54 top, 56 bottom, 61, 72, 77, 80 top, 81, 83, 92, 94 by JANE RUFFIN

Pages 1, 36 top left by ANN B. SWENGEL

Pages 4, 14, 15 top left and top right, 36 top right, 36 bottom, 40, 47 bottom, 62 bottom, 75, 96 (left and right), 97, 98 right, 99 right, 100 left by GEYATA AJILVSGI

Pages 6, 7, 45, 87, 91, 98 left, 101 by PATRICIA T. SUTTON

Pages 10, 12, 48, 55, 57 top, 63 bottom, 65, 66, 82 top by ALICE YARBOROUGH

Pages 15 bottom, 69 top and bottom, 70 top, 79, 86 by JUDYWHITE

Pages 37, 43 bottom, 71 top, 100 right by EVI BUCKNER

Page 38 by ALAN L. DETRICK

Page 39 by C. COLSTON BURRELL

Pages 41, 49 bottom, 50 bottom, 52, 58 top and bottom, 60, 68, 74, 78, 85 by LAUREN SPRINGER

Pages 42 top, 43 top, 49 top, 50 top, 57 bottom, 67, 71 bottom, 90, 93, 95 by DENISE GIBBS

Pages 42 bottom, 51, 59, 62 top, 63 top, 73 bottom, 76, 99 left by ANDY & SALLY WASOWSKI

Pages 46, 73 top by CHRISTINE M. DOUGLAS

Pages 54 bottom, 82 bottom, 84, 89 by P.A. OPLER

Pages 56 top, 64, 70 bottom, 80 bottom, 88 by ROGER L. HAMMER

CONTRIBUTORS

GEYATA AJILVSGI contributed plant encyclopedia entries appropriate for the Southeast and Southwest. She is a botanist, writer, photographer and gardener. Her books include *Butterfly Gardening for the South* as well as *Wildflowers of Texas* and *Field Guide to the Butterflies of Texas*. Her work has appeared in numerous publications.

DENISE GIBBS, who contributed plant encyclopedia entries for the Mid-Atlantic, is a park naturalist in Montgomery County, Maryland. She creates butterfly gardens and owns and operates Wings and Wildflowers, a nursery specializing in native plants for butterflies and hummingbirds. She has written and lectured widely on butterfly gardening.

ROGER HAMMER contributed plant and butterfly encyclopedias entries appropriate for Florida. He is a naturalist with Metro-Dade Parks Department's Natural Areas Management Section, and the author of numerous articles on the flora and fauna of southern Florida.

ALCINDA LEWIS is the guest editor of this handbook and wrote the chapters "Garden 'Pubs' for Butterflies" and "Butterfly Biology for Gardeners." She is a biologist specializing in plant-animal interactions, most recently learning in butterflies. She was editor of the journal of the Denver Botanic Gardens and of *Insect Learning: Ecological and Evolutionary Perspectives* with D. Papaj. She has contributed to *Fine Gardening* and other publications.

RICHARD MIKULA, who contributed to the butterfly encyclopedia, owns and operates Hole-in-Hand Butterfly Farm in Hazleton, Pennsylvania. He also serves as a habitat consultant to butterfly gardens, aviaries and parks. He has lectured and written extensively on butterflies and butterfly gardening.

PAUL OPLER, who contributed to the butterfly encyclopedia and regional lists, is a leading authority on North American butterflies. He has written several books, including *Butterflies East of the Great Plains,* and was a major contributor to *Butterfly Gardening* (Xerces Society). He has been vice-president of the Xerces Society and is currently with the National Biological Survey.

JANE RUFFIN contributed plant encyclopedia entries appropriate to the

Northeast. She is a naturalist and photographer whose work appears in numerous publications. She lectures on butterfly gardening and does workshops on butterflies and photography. She is the author of *Where Are the Butterfly Gardens?* She has been a volunteer in the Entomology Department of the Academy of Natural Sciences in Philadelphia since 1985.

SANDY RUSSELL contributed plant encyclopedia entries appropriate to California. She served as a teacher/naturalist at an Audubon center in Connecticut and the Charmelee Nature Preserve in Malibu, California, where she recently designed an educational butterfly garden. She brings live butterflies and caterpillars to a wide variety of school groups, garden clubs and art associations.

LAUREN SPRINGER, who contributed plant encyclopedia entries appropriate to the Rocky Mountains, is the author/photographer of *Water-Wise Gardening* and *The Undaunted Garden.* She writes an award-winning gardening column for *The Denver Post* and grows more than 1,000 plant species, some new to cultivation, in her northern Colorado garden.

PATRICIA SUTTON contributed to the plant and butterfly encyclopedias. She is teacher/naturalist at the New Jersey Audubon Society's Cape May Bird Observatory. She wrote *Backyard Habitat for Birds: A Guide for Landowners and Communities in New Jersey* (Project Flightpath: Backyard Habitat for Birds and other Wildlife in New Jersey) and co-authored *How to Spot an Owl* with her husband, Clay Sutton.

ANN SWENGEL, who contributed plant encyclopedia entries appropriate for the Midwest, is summer naturalist at Mirror Lake State Park in Wisconsin. She conducts research on prairie and lupine-associated butterflies, accounts of which have appeared in *American Butterflies.* She is actively involved in education about butterflies, in part through her activities in the North American Butterfly Association.

ALICE YARBOROUGH wrote the chapter "Designing Gardens for Butterflies" and contributed plant encyclopedia entries appropriate for the Pacific Northwest . She has contributed articles and photography on butterfly gardening to *Fine Gardening* magazine and *The Butterfly Garden* by Jerry Sedenko. Her article "Gardening for Wildlife" appears in the new *Taylor Master Guide to Gardening.*

HARDINESS ZONE MAP

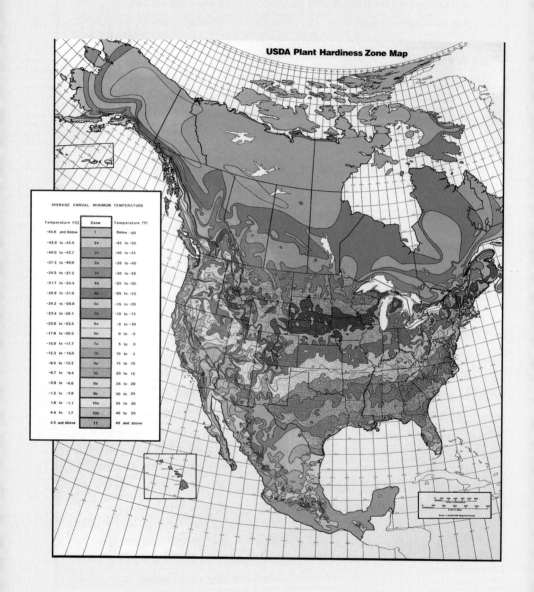

USDA Plant Hardiness Zone Map

AVERAGE ANNUAL MINIMUM TEMPERATURE

Temperature (°C)	Zone	Temperature (°F)
-45.6 and Below	1	Below -50
-42.8 to -45.5	2a	-45 to -50
-40.0 to -42.7	2b	-40 to -45
-37.3 to -40.0	3a	-35 to -40
-34.5 to -37.2	3b	-30 to -35
-31.7 to -34.4	4a	-25 to -30
-28.9 to -31.6	4b	-20 to -25
-26.2 to -28.8	5a	-15 to -20
-23.4 to -26.1	5b	-10 to -15
-20.6 to -23.3	6a	-5 to -10
-17.8 to -20.5	6b	0 to -5
-15.0 to -17.7	7a	5 to 0
-12.3 to -15.0	7b	10 to 5
-9.5 to -12.2	8a	15 to 10
-6.7 to -9.4	8b	20 to 15
-3.9 to -6.6	9a	25 to 20
-1.2 to -3.8	9b	30 to 25
1.6 to -1.1	10a	35 to 30
4.4 to 1.7	10b	40 to 35
4.5 and Above	11	40 and Above

INDEX

Gardening Books for the Next Century from the Brooklyn Botanic Garden

Don't miss any of the gardening books in Brooklyn Botanic Garden's 21st-Century Gardening Series! Published four times a year, these acclaimed books explore the frontiers of ecological gardening—offering practical, step-by-step tips on creating environmentally sensitive and beautiful gardens for the 1990s and the new century. Your subscription to BBG's 21st-Century Gardening Series is free with Brooklyn Botanic Garden membership.

SUBSCRIPTIONS

Please photocopy this form, complete and return to:
Brooklyn Botanic Garden, 1000 Washington Avenue, Brooklyn, NY 11225-1099.

Your name...

Address...

City/State/Zip..Phone...

AMOUNT

☐ Yes, I want to subscribe to the 21st-Century Gardening Series (4 quarterly volumes) by becoming a member of the Brooklyn Botanic Garden:

☐ $35 (Subscriber)   ☐ $125 (Signature)

☐ $50 (Family/Dual)   ☐ $300 Sponsor)   ....

☐ Enclosed is my tax-deductible contribution to the Brooklyn Botanic Garden.   ....

TOTAL   ....

Form of payment: ☐ Check enclosed ☐ Visa ☐ Mastercard

Credit card# ....Exp ....Signature ....

FOR INFORMATION ON ORDERING ANY OF THE FOLLOWING BACK TITLES, PLEASE WRITE THE BROOKLYN BOTANIC GARDEN AT THE ABOVE ADDRESS OR CALL (718) 622-4433, EXT. 274.

American Cottage Gardening
Annuals: A Gardener's Guide
Bonsai: Special Techniques
Culinary Herbs
Dyes from Nature
The Environmental Gardener
Ferns
Garden Photography
The Gardener's World of Bulbs
Gardening for Fragrance
Gardening in the Shade
Gardening with Wildflowers
 & Native Plants
Going Native: Biodiversity

in Our Own Backyards
Greenhouses & Garden Rooms
Growing Fruits
Herbs & Cooking
Herbs & Their Ornamental Uses
Hollies: A Gardener's Guide
Indoor Bonsai
Japanese Gardens
Native Perennials
The Natural Lawn & Alternatives
Natural Insect Control
A New Look at Vegetables
A New Look at Houseplants
Orchids for the Home

 & Greenhouse
Ornamental Grasses
Perennials: A Gardener's Guide
Pruning Techniques
Roses
Salad Gardens
Shrubs: The New Glamour Plants
Soils
The Town & City Gardener
Trees: A Gardener's Guide
Water Gardening
The Winter Garden
Woodland Gardens: Shade
 Gets Chic